THE WITHERING AWAY
OF THE CITY

THE WITHERING AWAY
OF THE CITY

YORK WILLBERN

1964

UNIVERSITY OF ALABAMA PRESS

Copyright 1964 by the University of Alabama Press

Library of Congress Catalog Card Number 63-19642

Manufactured in the United States of America by
Birmingham Printing Company, Birmingham, Ala.

PREFACE

THE INSTITUTIONS AND PROCESSES OF GOVERNMENT are inescapably related to the techniques and patterns of living of the populations with which they are concerned. These patterns of life are always changing, but the pace of change in urban America has been particularly rapid in the current generation. Most of us are so deeply immersed in these transformations that we do not understand their nature very well, and we see even less clearly the governmental adaptations that will be associated with changes in living patterns. In the realm of public policy, second perhaps only to the challenges of international relations in a nuclear age are the challenges of providing tolerable and attractive conditions of life in our growing urban agglomerations. These essays are an attempt to describe and speculate about some of the developments in governmental institutions and processes related to changes in urban life.

This volume is based upon lectures delivered at the University of Alabama in November, 1961. For nearly twenty years, a similar group of lectures has been given there each fall as a part of the Southern Regional Training Program in Public Administration. The quality of the volumes which have resulted from these lectures is certainly so high that it is both a great honor and a real challenge to be invited to participate in the series.

It was a very special privilege and pleasure for me to have the opportunity to give the SRTP lectures in 1961. I had been myself a part of that enterprise, as a member of the faculty of the University of Alabama, from 1946 to 1957, and it was particularly rewarding to feel again the warmth and the stimulation of the institution and the Program. I am grateful to Robert B. Highsaw and Coleman B. Ransone, Jr., my hosts, for the opportunity to present the lectures and for their hospitality while my wife and I were in Tuscaloosa.

York Willbern
Bloomington, Indiana
September, 1963

CONTENTS

"When a man is tired of London, he is tired of life; for there is in London all that life can afford."

Samuel Johnson

Quoted by Thomas P. Peardon, *The Urban Problems,* Supplement to *Political Science Quarterly,* XXVII (May, 1960), iii.

"What can 'town' mean, when the municipality is merely a strip on an endless cluttered highway, with only signs declaring 'You Are Now Leaving . . .' and 'You Are Now Entering . . .' to serve as divisions between one incandescent nightmare and its adjoining twin?"

Dan Jacobson

Quoted in a book review by Donald Malcolm in *The New Yorker,* XXXVII, No. 17 (June 10, 1961), 132.

Chapter 1

THE TRANSFORMATION OF
THE URBAN COMMUNITY

THE LINGUISTIC AND HISTORICAL RELATIONSHIPS BE-tween the words "city" and "civilization" have often been noted. The present state of American cities and that great part of the civilization of this country which revolves around their functioning and well-being, have provoked a rapidly growing volume of interest and concern.

Most literate people are reasonably familiar with the gross outlines of urban population movements. They know that urban areas have increased in population much more rapidly than rural areas, that the great bulk of this growth has been in areas of metropolitan character, and that suburban areas have been growing much more rapidly than have central cities. None of us, however, yet understands adequately the implications and consequences of these massive redistributions of the population.

We are participating, in my opinion, in two revolutions, one imposed upon the other, and the meaning of the second is partially obscured by the fact that the first, much older, revolution is continuing even as the second develops.

The first of these revolutions, of course, is the rise of an urban way of life. The second is its diffusion and dispersal over the countryside. The first has been in the making in Europe and in this country for several hundred years. It was in nearly full flower when Johnson and Boswell were enjoying the fleshpots of eighteenth century London. This revolution was based on the rise of trade and on the growth of industry. The new technologies which promoted specialization, manufacturing, and great increases in the interchange of goods and services have continued and been accelerated in the last two generations. They are now world-wide in their impact; the non-Western world as well as the West is struggling today with the gains and costs of these changes. Those who are staggered by the problems of urbanization in this country are really shaken when they see Tokyo or Calcutta. Tokyo, the world's most populous city, has no sewerage for eighty percent of the metropolitan area. In Calcutta two-thirds of a million people have no home but the public streets and alleys.[1]

These urbanizing forces continue unabated in this country. The proportion of the national population living in areas defined by the Census Bureau as "metropolitan" increased from 58 percent in 1950 to 63 percent in 1960. The proportions continue to

[1] *New York Times,* Dec. 17, 1961, p. 40; Paul N. Ylvisaker, address to the World Traffic Engineering Conference, Washington, D. C., Aug. 21, 1961.

grow and will probably reach 70 or 75 percent before the Census Bureau decides that it is unable any longer to fabricate definitions to demarcate a population which is almost universally metropolitanized.

The second revolution is much newer and has been much more strongly felt in this country than anywhere else. This is the outward explosion of our urban centers. It has several causes, of course. One is the desire of families, particularly families with children, for detached dwellings on substantial plots of land. Sir Frederic J. Osborn, dean of British planners and editor of *Town and Country Planning,* emphasized this desire in a recent address to American planning officials, and in so doing raised a question of crucial importance to the continuation and welfare of large cities. He indicated that the most disastrous shortcoming associated with city size is "the lack of sufficient space inside cities for good family dwellings with private yards or gardens, for recreation, for industrial efficiency, and for the vegetative surroundings and the quiet and simple beauty man needs and desires for the fullness of life."

Relative unconsciousness of this aspect of the urban problem surprises me in all countries, including my own, because the most conspicuous cause of the "metropolitan explosion" is the spontaneous quest by more and more urban families, as net incomes rise, for the family house standing in its own yard. The outward movement of the well-off is nothing new; what is new is the spread of wealth to far more numerous classes who can afford what Susannah's husband provided for her in Babylon and great senators took for themselves in ancient Rome—a suburban home in a garden. . . . such environments reflect a universal natural desire that man indulges wherever and whenever he becomes prosperous and free.

Admittedly, there are some genuine addicts of high urban culture to whom space and green surroundings make little appeal—types who like to live in city centres with their rich assemblies of theatres, concert halls, art galleries, restaurants, night clubs, snack bars, and hamburger stands—and are reassured by the bustle of crowds, traffic noises, flashing signs, and the insistent impact on their senses of commercial vitality. I do not deplore the existence of these types, though I suspect that their contribution to our culture is over valued. But they are a tiny minority. . . .[2]

This view is, of course, greatly at odds with that suggested by Mrs. Jane Jacobs in a book which is currently attracting a great deal of attention among students of urbanism.[3] If the figures on population movement are an accurate indication of the desires of people for home environments, the evidence certainly supports Sir Frederic's view much more strongly than that of Mrs. Jacobs.

A good many technological developments have made this dispersion of urban housing relatively easy. Reliance upon electric power and the ease of power transmission, telephone lines, septic tanks and similar developments bring to widely scattered houses many of the conveniences and amenities once possible only in very closely settled cities.

A development of social technology—the long-term, monthly payment mortgage loan with low in-

[2] Frederic J. Osborn, "The Conqueror City," *Town and Country Planning,* XXIX (Apr., 1961), 141.
[3] Jane Jacobs, *The Death and Life of Great American Cities* (New York: Random House, 1961).

terest rates—has greatly facilitated the spread of American families into single-family detached dwellings. The growth of credit arrangements of this type has certainly been encouraged and fostered by national legislation. It can be argued that the nature of the urban residential patterns of this generation has been shaped very substantially by FHA and similar governmental programs. The overwhelming political support for these programs, however, and the existence of parallel non-governmental developments indicate clearly that these credit socialization devices have probably been more the product than the cause of the social and economic forces at work.

If the basic desire for detached dwellings and space is one cause of the dispersion, another and very important cause is the appearance and practically universal use of the automobile in this country. We now have available, for most individuals, personalized rapid transit. The customary reaction to the automobile of Mrs. Jacobs and others who admire the congestion of dense urban settlement is to wish it would go away.

The impact of the automobile revolution is newer than many of us realize; its outlines are only now beginning to emerge. The last decade was the first in which it was fully operative; the 1960 census returns gave figures which indicate some of the results on a nation-wide basis. Automobiles began to be widespread in the 1920's, but too little time had as yet passed for really basic changes in ways of living and spatial relationships. In the 1930's the great economic depression overshadowed and hampered adjustments to the new technology; the 1940's brought another overpowering circumstance, the war and its aftermath, to mask and postpone the basic changes. They hit us full force in the 1950's, but a decade is a short time for a social revolution. The greatest public works enterprise in the history of mankind, our national system of expressways, which will probably give the automobile age its greatest boost since the Model T Ford, is just beginning. I am indebted to Harlan Cleveland for a statistic which he considered the most interesting of a recent year: we now have enough automotive vehicles in operation in this country for every man, woman, and child in the population to ride comfortably and simultaneously in the front seats.

It is difficult for us to realize that this new revolution may have a social impact comparable to that of the first. The basic purpose of a city is the facilitation of interchange—the interchange of goods through trade and merchandising, of labor and services in industrial and service enterprises, of messages and ideas in financial and political and cultural activities. When the means of interchange are drastically altered, the nature of the city must also be drastically altered.

In the large cities of a century ago, population was tightly concentrated. Concentration was necessary, in order for people to get from home to work and school and shop and engage in the other complex exchanges of a city. When each individual and

most of the goods move from place to place within
the urban environment in a vehicle weighing more
than a ton and capable of moving economically at
the rate of a mile a minute, the old patterns of settlement are technologically obsolete and will inevitably
be changed. To achieve for a given population the
same facility of circulation that the older concentrated cities had for pedestrian, horse-drawn, or even
rail traffic, the modern city requires a land area many
times greater. When movement and interchange were
pedestrian and horse-drawn, an efficient area for a
population of 200,000 might be about four square
miles;[4] for 200,000 people now, on a one or two
persons per car basis (increasingly the normal pattern), the most efficient area might well be 100
square miles.

Many of the great cities of the world outside the
United States are experiencing the integrating revolution, with relatively little evidence yet of the disintegrating one. Perhaps they may avoid the second.
A Soviet economist, watching Americans coming to
work one-in-a-car is supposed to have said "we'll
never make that mistake—that is, if we can help it."[5]

In this country, however, disintegrating forces are
moving at a rapid pace. The area north of the Ohio
River and east from Chicago and St. Louis contains
the urban heart of the United States. There were in
this area in 1950 a dozen cities with more than half

[4] In 1850 Philadelphia had a population of 121,000 and an area of
two square miles.
[5] Ylvisaker, p. 18.

a million inhabitants each. What happened to the population of these cities in the decade of the 1950's, a decade in which urbanization continued apace? Every one of them lost, rather than gained, in population. While the urban area, the metropolitan area, in each case grew very substantially in population, not a single one of the large central cities in this area increased. If this is what is happening to the oldest, best established American cities, will Birmingham and Indianapolis, or even Houston and Los Angeles, be far behind?

The famous Regional Plan of 1929 for the New York metropolitan area projected a population by 1965 of 21 million people living in approximately 1,000 square miles of the region. In 1960, five years before the projected date, there were actually only

CHANGE IN POPULATION, 1950-1960, MAJOR CITIES IN
NORTHEAST AND MIDWEST

	1950	1960	Amount Change
Baltimore	949,708	939,024	— 10,684
Boston	801,444	697,197	—104,247
Buffalo	580,132	532,759	— 47,373
Chicago	3,620,962	3,550,404	— 70,558
Cincinnati	503,998	502,550	— 1,448
Cleveland	914,808	876,050	— 38,758
Detroit	1,849,568	1,670,144	—179,424
New York	7,891,957	7,781,984	—109,973
Philadelphia	2,071,605	2,002,512	— 69,093
Pittsburgh	676,806	604,332	— 72,474
St. Louis	856,796	750,026	—106,770
Washington, D.C.	802,178	763,956	— 38,222

Source: *Statistical Abstract of the United States,* 1962, pp. 22-23.

16 million people, but the urbanized area constituted 2,000 square miles, twice the projected
amount.[6]

The most recent major study of the New York
metropolitan area, which Raymond Vernon and his
associates made for the same Regional Plan Association, came to the following conclusion:

As one surveys the outward shift of the population in the New
York Metropolitan Region and of the consumer activities tied
to them, the forces behind the shift seem near-inexorable.
Basic technological developments in transportation and deep-
seated changes in consumer wants appear to lie behind the
phenomenon. Here and there one sees evidences of prefer-
ences which breast the main tide; the occasional reappearance
of a disillusioned exurbanite in his former city haunts, the
gradual growth of apartments-in-the-city for the very rich—
these are phenomena whose impact cannot be overlooked.
The bigger risk, however, is that their implications for the
future will be exaggerated rather than overlooked. Short of
some fundamental alteration in consumer outlook or in urban
environment, the trends for the future seem likely to represent a continuation—even a speed up—of the dispersive
tendencies of the past.[7]

This is what they predict in the text of the book.
After coming to this conclusion, however, Mr. Vernon inspected the 1960 census returns and found
that he had been short of the mark. The city core
has declined in population more than he anticipated,

[6] Paul Windels, "The Region—Past, Present, and Future," *Metropolis 1985*, p. 21, a report from a conference held at Arden House,
March 1, 1961.
[7] Raymond Vernon, *Metropolis 1985* (Cambridge: Harvard University
Press, 1960), p. 165.

and the outlying areas have expanded more rapidly. In a footnote attached after the report was completed, but before the volume was finally published, he confessed that "in general, the dispersive population forces in the Region seem even stronger than those built into our model."[8]

Even the census figures summarizing the growth in the outlying portions of metropolitan areas and the losses or much slower growth in the urban core may understate the dispersion. For example, the Census Bureau defines the Indianapolis metropolitan area as Marion County. This area increased in population by 24 percent between 1950 and 1960, a very substantial rate of growth. But the counties immediately to the north, east, south, and west of Marion County, not included in the census-defined metropolitan area, had rates of growth of 40, 30, 67, and 65 percent, respectively. The growth of these counties immediately beyond the census metropolitan area limits is not considered in the statistics to be suburban growth, but the percentage growth has often been even greater than that of the suburban areas *within* the official metropolitan area.

During the decades when the urbanizing forces were strongest, and before the forces of dispersal had begun to accumulate, the percentage of the population living in the central city of an urbanizing area increased substantially. This percentage has tended to decrease as the second revolution has become mixed with the first. In the accompanying chart are

[8] *Ibid.,* p. 222.

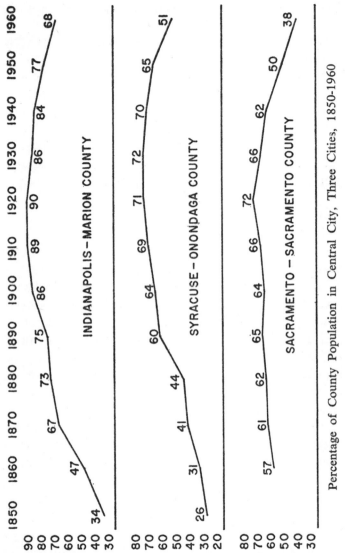

Percentage of County Population in Central City, Three Cities, 1850-1960

some representative figures from three cities at which I have been looking intensively.

In each of the three cities the central city reached its peak percentage in 1920 or 1930, along with the initial surge of the automobile revolution, and has since declined at a rapid and ordinarily accelerating rate. New York City constituted the largest percentage, in population, of the counties composing its metropolitan area in *1910*; the percentage has been dropping ever since. The peak in Birmingham was *1930*.

In gross national figures the greatest concentration of metropolitan population inside central cities occurred between 1920 and 1930. Until 1920 the central cities were growing faster than their metropolitan rings; beginning with the census of 1930, the fringe growth has been faster than the central growth, and the gap widens with each census. During the 1950-1960 decade, the central cities of the 212 metropolitan areas of the country increased 1.5 percent in population within their 1950 boundaries, and added another 9.2 percent by annexation, for a total increase of 10.7 percent, and, as I have indicated, many of the biggest and oldest actually lost population. The remaining, or fringe portion of the metropolitan areas, increased 48.6 percent. The more than ninety percent of the land area outside the metropolises saw its population increase by eleven percent.

It is roughly accurate to say that one-third of the American population is within the central cities of metropolitan areas, and this segment is increasing at the rate of one percent per year, almost entirely by annexation. (This increase, as we shall see, is concentrated in a few states.) Another third is in the metropolitan fringes, and here the rate of increase is four percent per year, in spite of the bites taken from it by annexation into the central cities. The remaining third of the population is in the rest of the country, and this segment also is increasing at the rate of about one percent per year.

Nor is this diffusion of urban life over the countryside to be limited by the commuting range, expanding though that range may be through massive expenditures on expressways. We are not witnessing a pattern in which people seek out spaciousness for living, but return to a congested core each day for work. The jobs also seek space, and manufacturers want space as well as home builders.

In recent years, manufacturers in the New York Metropolitan Region have dramatically increased their use of land. Our surveys indicate that the amount of plot space per worker in the post war suburban plants of the Region is over four times as great as in suburban plants built before 1922. In the new plants more than an acre of land is used for every ten workers.[9]

The service activities, of course, follow the population. The spectacular growth of shopping centers, the great demands for extensive sites for new schools, the need to locate all kinds of enterprises where there is ample parking space, are indications of dispersion

[9] *Ibid.*, pp. 116-117.

in economic activity. Even in New York, which has peculiar reasons for concentration because its central business district serves in large measure as the central business district of the nation, the jobs are moving out about as fast as the people, according to the Vernon studies.[10] Frank W. Herring, Deputy Director of Comprehensive Planning of the Port of New York Authority, says that "growth in journey-to-work travel is no longer focused on the Central Business District, but rather is characterized by inter-suburban travel, reverse commuting and the like."[11]

The net flow of commuting is, of course, still toward the center, and it will probably continue to be for a long time. The Vernon studies indicate that the core of the New York area now has about half the population of the region and two-thirds of the jobs. According to their projections, by 1985 the core will have only one-third the population but will probably still have half the jobs.

The dispersion of employment may be greater in other centers than in New York. In the Chicago area (where the city of Chicago constitutes a larger portion of its metropolitan area than does New York),

[10] New York is to be contrasted to London and Tokyo, its two largest competitors as world urban centers. In both of these, the population increase is at the edges while the jobs continue to be relatively concentrated in the center. Paul Ylvisaker reports that land in the heart of Tokyo is four times as expensive as land in the heart of Manhattan. The chief reason for the difference is almost certainly the difference in the state of the automotive revolution.

[11] "Metropolitan Growth and Metropolitan Travel Patterns," a paper presented at the annual meeting of the Highway Research Board, Committee on Urban Research, Jan. 12, 1961.

the city's share of manufacturing employment in the area fell from 84 percent in 1920 to 81 percent in 1940 and to 72 percent in 1957.[12] A continuation of this accelerating trend would suggest that the city of Chicago now has less than 70 percent of the industrial jobs in the area, compared to about 58 percent of the people.

Dispersal of manufacturing activity from the inner zones of the central city was the dominant trend in plant location throughout the United States in 1950-1960. In Chicago, typically, the greatest gains in activity took place in an arc ten to fifteen miles from the central business district. The greatest losses occurred within five miles of the core. Warehouses, in particular, moved from inner zones to the periphery, situating themselves close to areas of population growth and expanded manufacturing activity. To call this process suburbanization may be too much of a simplification.[13]

In many cities of smaller size, the great developments in industrialization, and in jobs, occur beyond the city limits. The new industries tend to locate in industrial parks, or on spacious sites well outside the cities. In Syracuse, New York, for example, the city's proportion of the population of Onondaga County has been declining for more than twenty years, but its proportion of the assessed valuation of the county has been declining even more rapidly

[12] Northeastern Illinois Metropolitan Area Planning Commission, *Social Geography of Metropolitan Chicago* (Chicago, 1960), p. 20.
[13] Mark Reinsberg, *Growth and Change in Metropolitan Areas and Their Relation to Metropolitan Transportation: A Research Summary* (Evanston, Ill.: The Transportation Center, Northwestern University, 1961), p. 10.

than its proportion of the population, indicating that productive property, which has higher assessments than residences, has been growing faster outside the city than inside.[14]

Some observers argue that the tide of movement out of central cities into suburban and rurban areas can be checked and reversed by improved mass transit, renewal of the older urban areas, and various other remedial measures. Efforts in this direction may be expected to continue. It seems likely that policy changes may affect the character of the movement somewhat, but the overwhelming bulk of the evidence makes the outward movement seem, as Vernon and his associates put it in their study of New York, "inexorable."

Most of our accumulated physical capital is in urban areas. The sweeping changes in the technology of settlement and interchange which have resulted in the shifting populations have a great impact on the maintenance and utility of these accumulated investments. The existence of these great investments, both in physical facilities and in skills and habits, constitutes a great drag upon adaptation to technological innovation. Farm homes and land holdings and habits of work have continued long after becoming technologically obsolescent; this is the basic cause of our so-called "farm problem." We now have similar lags because of the investments in outmoded urban plants. We live, however, in a relatively affluent age, an age when we can make mas-

[14] Roscoe C. Martin, Frank Munger, and others, *Decisions in Syracuse* (Bloomington: Indiana University Press, 1961), pp. 23 and 29.

sive continuing new investments, even at the price of losing full use of much of the old. Furthermore, our society is increasingly mobile, not only geographically but in capacity to shift patterns of behavior. Substitution of investment for many reasons, in addition to the changing technology of communication and movement, goes on continually.

With new investments being made as a matter of course, the investors (whether in productive plant, or in patterns of service, or in housing and ways of life) are able to locate in better conformity to the technological patterns of the present and future. The pressures to maintain and adapt and renew the center which have characterized European cities for many generations are far less demanding here. A merchant who sees opportunities for growth in an expanding urban environment, and who has or can get capital to invest, is much less likely to use it in rebuilding or refurnishing and improving a downtown store location. Instead he will join a new regional shopping center near a freeway interchange where there can be six square feet of parking space for every square foot of selling space.

So far, in this country the forces of the second, suburbanizing revolution have been balanced in large measure by the continuing forces of the first, urbanizing revolution. The massive forces for dispersal of investment have been accompanied by such great need for the use of all the possible capital available in urban areas that both the new and much of the old have been necessary.

The physical decay and obsolescence of the older

investment have not yet resulted in great decreases in property values. In the last thirty years the rate of investment in new housing units and new industrial and business sites in urban areas has not exceeded the rate of influx from the remote rural communities. To be more explicit, although over a million housing units a year have been built in urban fringe areas for the last decade, as yet comparatively few vacancies have appeared in the deteriorating housing units of the central cities. The new units serve as additions to the total urban supply, not as replacements. The accumulated overcrowding of the depression and war years and the continuing immigration from rural parts of the country have kept the demand for housing units at a sufficient intensity that rental income from slum property is still highly remunerative. As fast as the inhabitants of the gray area (or "mice country," as Robert Wood calls it) have moved out to the suburbs, the Negro, Puerto Rican, and hill country farm people have crowded in to the decaying houses of the old city. Reductions in population of the central cities, now definitely begun, have made it possible so far only to clear some land to provide more room for automobiles to maneuver and be stored and to reduce somewhat the doubling up and overcrowding; vacancy rates in slum housing are still not high enough to worry the landlords.

There are some indications that new housing construction has begun to catch up with the urban population growth. As to the deteriorating central city housing in New York, Vernon suggests that "no projection which we would consider realistic contemplates an increase in the demand for such housing in the Region anywhere near as great as the prospective increase in supply."[15] If vacancies in the slums begin to mount (as is already true in some decaying commercial and industrial properties) reductions in income potential may cause the values of the decaying central city properties to fall significantly.

Some forces do exist which tend to offset the disintegrating effects of transportation changes and the desire of people for detached dwellings. One is the great value for many small enterprises of what the economists call "external economies." These are the specialist services which a large enterprise may provide for itself but which a small enterprise can best get from other suppliers. Although these may be interchanged even in a dispersed, less congested locational pattern, there remain some advantages in the greater proximity of denser locations.

Second, and much more important, some activities in our complex society are best carried on where there is frequent and convenient opportunity for face-to-face contact with a variety of other people: the financial institutions, for example; the central corporate offices; the advertising business. Here, intelligence is perhaps the chief item of exchange, and it can best be exchanged on the basis of frequent conferences, luncheons, and personal contacts. For

[15] Vernon, p. 154.

this reason the shining towers of central Manhattan continue to rise although much of the surrounding area is deteriorating.

The central business district of New York has peculiar advantages, of course, because it performs so many of these functions for the whole nation and even the world. At the same time, the proportion of our society engaged in the white-collar, highly interpersonal communication activities is increasing so extensively that there are good economic prospects for the core of central business districts of many of our cities, even though the fabrication and distribution of goods may be continually dispersed.

Third, some industries need large quantities of relatively low-wage labor. Since the lowest income groups tend to live in the central city, and relatively near the center, and since these groups are somewhat less mobile, it is sometimes advantageous for lower-wage industries to stay near the population and transit center. In Chicago the industries showing the lowest decentralizing tendencies (though even here the net movement was outward) were textiles and apparel, lumber and furniture, and food products, all of which are comparatively low-wage operations.[16]

A fourth centralizing factor may be suggested, but its actual impact is not easy to predict. This is the almost certain great increase in the number of two-house families. Two-car families are now commonplace in this country, and two-house families are

[16] Reinsberg, pp. 18-19.

expected to become so. Already perhaps a million of the fifty million family units have more than one place of residence, and these million tend to be the high-income, high-status families whose patterns of life are copied by others as quickly as they can afford it. If one residence offers almost complete isolation, many families may plump in favor of the attractions and conveniences of high-density living for the other residence and use their automobiles as much or more for week-end as for daily commuting. The apparent preference of people with children for detached dwellings, however, along with the continually growing reliance upon the automobile even for frequent movements during the day, leads to considerable doubt that the rise in dual dwellings will result in more than a marginal integrating force.

How much can public policy shape and guide and direct these patterns of investment and of settlement? Was it government's cheap land policy which led to the rapid agricultural expansion of the early nineteenth century, or did migration and settlement force the government to follow the policy it did? Was it governmental promotion of the transcontinental railroads later in the century, and the Panama Canal early in this century, that linked the two coasts into an economic unit, or did the economic ties and links make the governmental public works enterprises necessary? Was it the massive public water system that made possible the settlement of so many people in and around New York, and the development and operation of the subway system that enabled them to focus such a concentration of economic activity in Manhattan, or were these great public enterprises produced rather haltingly to meet the necessities of the developing situation? No simple answer is possible to such chicken-and-egg priority questions, but recent searching economic studies of metropolitan regions suggest very strongly that, as Charles Adrian summarizes it:

Both local and regional (metropolitan) governments tend to follow the economic pattern rather than to lead it. Governmental innovations that complement the decisions of the market place are likely to succeed; others are not.[17]

The British have had the urbanizing revolution for a longer period and to a greater degree than we have, and the early waves of a flood of urban dispersal (they call it urban sprawl) are apparent in England today. Between 1952 and 1960 the population of the London conurbation decreased by 139,000, while the population of the twenty to thirty mile wide belt encircling the conurbation increased by 765,000. But only the people are moving out—not the jobs. The center gained 260,000 jobs while losing 140,000 residents; the fringe gained only 200,000 jobs while acquiring 750,000 inhabitants.[18] The British planners have urged, and partially implemented, a national policy to combat both

[17] Charles R. Adrian, "Metropology: Folklore and Field Research," *Public Administration Review,* XXI (Summer, 1961), 155.
[18] "The London Region and the Development of South East England, 1961 to 1981," *Town and Country Planning,* XXIX (June, 1961), 225.

the congestion of the center and the sprawl of the cutting edges. They propose to constrict the central metropolis with an encircling green belt and to take care of the "over spill" in new towns—either completely new or planned new developments around old but small centers. The density of the great central cities is gradually to be reduced. Each of the new towns is to be relatively self-contained, with jobs for the inhabitants, trade and service establishments to care for their needs, appropriate community facilities, and adequate housing, all located within a space convenient to pedestrian or bicycle mobility. To keep this convenience of access, the new towns are to have firm limits as to size, and while most houses will be single-family with small garden spaces, residential densities will be substantially higher than in most American suburban developments.

Many American planners favor exploring similar programs in this country, but they are hampered by great technological and economic obstacles. Whatever the case in Britain, it is difficult to foresee here a relationship between place of residence and place of employment stable enough to make the self-contained, small-city concept a viable one. American occupational and residential mobility creates too many opportunities for the worker to find more attractive employment in another city or in the central metropolis without moving his residence. Or he can find more attractive housing in another place without changing jobs. With the ubiquity of the automobile and the high-speed road, the population will not be "contained." Furthermore, the needs of the automobile for space will almost certainly dictate much more extensive patterns of land utilization than are foreseen by the British.

Even in Britain there are substantial doubts that the scheme can withstand the assault of growing affluence and motorization. Some big industrial establishments, located on the outskirts of the metropolitan areas, are recruiting workers in some of the new towns. This tendency, if pushed much further, may make of some of them bedroom suburbs for commuters. Some of the shopping centers in the new towns are so attractive that they draw automobile-borne customers from great distances around, and thus become regional shopping centers after the American pattern, but without the facilities for parking or traffic-handling. While the new town developments certainly have many attractions, political pressure has not been great enough to induce the government to build them at anything like the rate which the planners would like. And even in the green belts, though they have been relatively well protected, the pressures for land are so great that the rate of development and of population growth exceeds the national and the urban averages.

Whatever may be the situation in other countries, the evidence seems clear that in this country our farms and small towns are being abandoned in a great movement into an urban way of life. At the same time the city, in the sense of a tightly-knit corporate community with a clear distinction between its high-density living and the rural countryside, is fast becoming so blurred at the edges as to be incapable of operational definition. There seems little to block an endless expansion of urban or semi-urban ways of life over vast areas of the countryside outside our traditional city limits. Instead of distinct cities with distinguishable centers and edges somewhat like a fried egg, we seem likely to be approaching in large segments of our country a condition somewhat like that of a thin layer of scrambled eggs spread over much of the platter. The more urban we become, the more shaky become both the concept and the reality of the city.

Chapter 2

THE METROPOLITAN
PREDICAMENT

THE TRADITIONAL MODEL[1] OF LOCAL GOVERNMENT IN the United States envisions two different types of units of government. One type is territorial, the other, corporate.

The basic territorial unit is normally the county, although in some states the township has some of the same attributes and characteristics. These units are territorial in the sense that all of the territory of the state is divided into the units, and every citizen of the state normally resides within one of them. They are not voluntary; they are created by the state and imposed on the inhabitants of the area. Essentially they are territorial subdivisions of the state, convenient units into which many of the state's activities can be decentralized for purposes of administration and the most rudimentary policy-making.

---

[1] Models are, of course, simplifications, and there are many modifications and exceptions in actual practice. In this instance the oldest practices are those which conform least to the model. New England and Virginia have particularly significant differences.

These units are utilized for the application of many *state* policies and programs, even though many of the particular officers administering these policies and programs are chosen by *local* popular election. Some of these state programs are regulatory, some are service in character, but the general level of services supplied is minimal, designed primarily for rural patterns of life. Sometimes the governments of the units are allowed some discretion in undertaking additional programs and services, but this discretion is ordinarily rather exceptional and limited.

The political and administrative organization of the government of these units is ordinarily particularistic and disintegrated. Since there is little conception of a corporate community, which undertakes activities on its own initiative and in its own behalf, there is little conception of an integrated process of public decision-making. Offices and agencies are established and organized independently; some of them are independently responsible to the electorate; others, particularly in the newer functional areas, tend to have citizen boards and strong ties with state administrative agencies. Although generally a rudimentary central governing body or council exists, it has very limited controls over most of the working governmental agencies. Ordinarily no such official as a central executive is even envisioned.

These territorial units are based on the fundamental assumption of a rural style of life, with only a limited necessity for governmental activities and services.

The corporate type of governmental unit is represented primarily by the city, of course, although the term town, or village, or borough is sometimes applied to the smaller units. (Names are not always revealing. In some northeastern states the town is a territorial unit, although it has mixed characteristics. In Alaska the territorial units corresponding most closely to counties are called boroughs.) These units are spotted over the landscape only in those areas where concentration or clustering of the population is sufficient to require a special level of services stemming from density of settlement. Although established and operated within a framework of state law, these units are essentially voluntary, formed on the initiative of the local residents and undertaking (within prescribed limits) whatever activities the local inhabitants wish to undertake. As an indication of their character as voluntary associations of individuals for their own purposes, these units are called corporations. (To suggest the contrast, the territorial units are frequently termed quasi-corporations.) The framework of government of a corporate unit is ordinarily determined in a charter, which is in considerable measure tailored to the wishes and needs of the incorporators or their successors.

These corporate governmental units, occupying only a very small fraction of the territory of any state, are suited to the historic phenomenon of the city, a concentrated clustering of inhabitants into a comparatively small, distinct, definable territory. They are designed to do in a corporate and collective fashion many of those things which are required in a congested population but which cannot be done adequately by individuals. Such concentrated services (and, in some measure, regulations) are confined to the geographical limits of the "incorporated" area and are paid for by the inhabitants of the area.

Since, generally speaking, the unit undertakes those services and activities needed and required by the inhabitants, and at a level and to a degree for which they are willing to pay, the political and administrative organization of the unit tends to be cohesive and integrated. Clearly, one need and requirement must be balanced against another in order that, just as the community itself is highly interrelated, the services and activities of its government may be appropriately interrelated. The governing body tends to have rather complete and thorough control over all of the governmental functions and activities, and ordinarily the executive function is lodged in a strong and distinct center.

Obviously such units are designed for an urban style of life.

What happens to the operation of this model when patterns of settlement change? When the far-flung subdivisions and the ribbons of development stretch out to great distances beyond and around the older concentrations? When an urban way of life begins to permeate great sections of the landscape instead of being confined to the "walls of the city"?

We retain the form of the corporate unit, but much of its rationale is disappearing. The city limits constitute an important legal boundary line even when sociologically and economically they seem to be relatively meaningless. On the assumption that the incorporation is a voluntary one, our laws normally provide that the limits can be extended to take in additional homes and businesses only with the consent of the particular segment being annexed. And new corporations may be formed by any group having the requisite characteristic of geographical contiguity, even though the area involved consists only of the homes of people and includes no places of employment or trade or social life.

Furthermore, even if an attempt were made to apply rational measurements to determine the appropriate extent of a municipal corporation it is difficult if not impossible to arrive at a defensible position, even at one point in time. The extent of the urban community is not the same for one purpose as it is for another. Upon occasion I have visited a relative in northeastern New Jersey who lives within sight of the Empire State Building upon those rare days when the wind blows the smog in the right direction. It would certainly appear appropriate to say that he lives within the New York City Metropolitan Area, yet he tells me that he and his wife go to Manhattan perhaps once a year. From my home in Bloomington, Indiana, I have occasion to go to Manhattan much more frequently than he. And I probably see the *New York Times* more often than he and know more about the campaign for mayor.

In the urban agglomeration from north of Boston down to Virginia there are now 31,000,000 people. They live in one place, work in another, shop in another, go to church in still another, read a newspaper printed in one place, have their milk delivered from a dairy located somewhere else. Another mass approaching ten million lives in equally dispersed form in southern California.

In defining metropolitan areas for census purposes, the Census Bureau after struggling with detailed definitions for years recently settled for the hardly logical but easily workable conclusion that, in most instances, a metropolitan area consists of any county in which there is a city of 50,000 population or more. Thus in California the portion of Yolo County directly across the river from the center of Sacramento, and in some respects just a continuation of the business district, is not a part of the Sacramento Standard Metropolitan Statistical Area. On the other hand most of the Mojave Desert and some massive, uninhabited mountain ranges form part of the metropolitan area of San Bernardino.

The existing corporate limits have little relationship to the needs or the actualities of governmental functions and services. The freeways, the public transit systems, the systems of water supply and sewage disposal, of drainage and flood control, of air pollution and milk inspection, are related little if at all to the areas included within the various voluntary incorporations of groups of geographically contiguous citizens. Cities maintain parks and playgrounds outside their limits, and people living outside the limits use parks and playgrounds inside. Water supply can be and sometimes is stopped at the city limits, but, more commonly, a city with a good water system sells water wherever it is economic to sell it —and the market may be good in many directions; in some states the state law insists that cities maintaining such public utilities have the same responsibility as other public utilities, including the obligation to serve all those who present themselves and are willing to pay. A man driving back and forth to work or to a store may drive over the streets of several "jurisdictions" and expose himself to the traffic regulation policy of each.

Meanwhile, the traditional territorial units have been thrust into new functions and activities because of the waves of urban invaders. Counties and townships have had to begin worrying about parks, and zoning, and garbage collection, and regular police patrols, and, in still occasional but growing instances, public housing and urban renewal. And as they become involved with these functions once urban in character, territorial units must mobilize themselves for local policy consideration and for administrative activities for which their traditional machinery is very poorly adapted. They become less and less an area for the application of certain disparate state functions and more of a unit for true local self-government, even though their organization fits such a role rather poorly.

When neither the existing corporate units nor the existing territorial units can be adequately adapted to perform needed or wanted functions, government frequently turns to another expedient, the special district.

Local government special districts in the United States are older than we tend to think, and they are created for a number of reasons, not all of which are related to the second revolution in urban form.[2] They do not fit exactly into the basic model of local government described earlier. Since they are ordinarily formed by the voluntary action of an interested group of citizens and since they limit their activities to a particular area desiring a special service or activity, they constitute a type of corporate unit. Almost universally, however, they confine themselves to a single function or a group of closely related functions.

The oldest, and probably most important, reason for the establishment of these districts is the desire to separate a particular function from the general political system. The special district is the most extreme manifestation of the almost universal desire for separateness and autonomy on the part of special constituency and clientele groups. Some of our sense of community *is* geographical, it is true, but increasing specialization of society and the organization and increasing strength of specialized interests lead some groups to feel stronger loyalty to a func-

[2] The best description and analysis of these units may be found in John C. Bollens, *Special District Governments in the United States* (Berkeley and Los Angeles: University of California Press, 1957).

tional community or activity than to a geographical one. Even where the general purpose unit, the city or the county, operates a special function, the particular clientele or constituency involved with that function tends to demand as much autonomy as possible. Autonomy strengthens the lines of particularistic responsibility and helps to avoid lines of responsibility running through the general political system. This is certainly a major reason for the separate organization of school districts.

A second reason for organizing special districts is the desire to escape some limitation (ordinarily fiscal) placed upon the general purpose units by the state. Where the state statutes or constitution provide limits upon property tax rates or upon permissible indebtedness, and a movement to undertake or expand some activity which would run athwart these limitations has strong political backing, setting up a special purpose unit is frequently the recourse. This unit is largely or completely independent of the older ones; the old limitations do not apply to it (or, if similar limits apply to special districts, the new unit now has a new start on the tax rate or the debt total). The desire to escape these fiscal limits explains the creation of a good many special districts which have the same geographic limits and the same constituency as corresponding multi-purpose units. Since developing patterns of urban settlement create or accentuate fiscal constrictions, this device for escaping or ameliorating some of the financial confines has become increasingly necessary.

Sometimes the special purpose unit is established because the government lacks a grant of power to undertake a particular activity. Counties and other territorial units are more apt to need this expedient than are municipalities, for counties traditionally have been less able to determine for themselves the things which they will do for their constituents.

Occasionally a multi-purpose unit of government has territorial limits which are not suitable for a particular function. Again, the answer is the special district, with more accurate territorial limits. The special district may be smaller in area than the existing county or township, or city, or it may be larger. Sometimes it is simply a different geographical limit that is needed, as when a drainage area or water supply area has natural boundaries which do not correspond to the boundaries of a general unit.

Shifts and transitions in urban growth patterns have tremendously accentuated this last reason for setting up special districts. To get a "municipal-type" service in a particular area without embarking upon the whole range of corporate municipal responsibilities, a special purpose district provides an easy and attractive arrangement. Furthermore, when it becomes apparent that some particular function or activity, such as water pollution or the development of regional parks, requires a larger area than can reasonably be encompassed within any existing jurisdictional boundary, the formation of a metropolitan sewer district, or regional park district, is hit upon.

The most numerous and strongly entrenched single purpose districts are the school districts. They were formed primarily for the first of the reasons mentioned above, to furnish autonomy. The school constituency has long been powerful enough and jealous enough of its special position to demand and secure separation from the general governmental machinery. At the same time, fiscal imbalances resulting from the continuous, restless shifting of population and taxable resources have a tremendous impact upon school districting arrangements, an impact which is closely involved with and related to the more general problems of governmental areas.

The diminishing relevance of municipal boundaries, the spotty and unanticipated entry of territorial units into urban governmental functions, and the growth of various kinds of special districts have greatly emphasized a confused and jumbled and disordered pattern of local government, particularly in the metropolitan areas where two-thirds of the American population now live and where three-fourths may be expected to live before the generation is out. A recent report of the Advisory Commission on Intergovernmental Relations concludes that "the local government pattern in metropolitan areas is unbelievably complex."[3] The Commission estimated that the 212 Standard Metropolitan Statistical Areas had in 1960 more than 17,000 local

[3] Advisory Commission on Intergovernmental Relations, *Governmental Structure, Organization, and Planning in Metropolitan Areas* (Washington: U. S. Government Printing Office, 1961), p. 13.

governments, with approximately 1,000 each in the New York and Chicago regions.

These numbers seem impressive, but it should not be thought that the metropolitan areas have governmental problems stemming peculiarly from their numbers of governmental jurisdictions. These areas, with nearly two-thirds of the nation's population, have only about one-fifth of the governmental units. Furthermore, the larger metropolitan areas tend to have fewer governmental units in comparison to their population than the smaller ones. If numbers of governmental units in proportion to population is the problem, it is not the urban sections of the country which are suffering; Nebraska is the state with the greatest number of units of government in the country.

What, then, is the metropolitan "problem" with which students and reformers are concerned? Are the governmental arrangements for our sprawling urban populations falling short of the needs? Are the residents of the metropolitan areas restive and unhappy with their lot?

Adding up the influences and coercions of the attracting and repelling forces, far more people seem to be voting in favor of metropolitan life than against it. The total populations of these areas continue to grow astonishingly, not only absolutely but relatively. In economic terms the average income and standard of living of the dwellers of the metropolitan areas are significantly higher than the national average. And even though the populations of the older

central cities are declining, great numbers of people
continue to move into them to replace most of the
emigrants, preferring even this congested environment to the inadequacy of the rural communities
from which they came. As Paul Ylvisaker put it:

Ask the least fortunate in any urban setting, affluent or
under-developed: the Negro ghettoed in New York or London, or the bustee walla of Old Delhi—ask whether he would
choose to return to the area from which he or his people
came, and the answer far more often than not is a revealing
No. . . . [The American metropolis] has been the agent of a
surprisingly peaceful revolution which has made a nation of
farmers into a nation of urbanites, broken up the single ghetto
of the Negro South into a liberating diffusion of dissolving
ghettos in far-flung cities across the country, and brought the
children of backwoods and backwater bondage into the main
stream of American life.[4]

Looking at the matter from a more limited perspective, the public services do operate. The machinery creaks and groans at times, but it does not
break down, and acceptable, "satisficing" expedients
seem always to be forthcoming. The tap can be
depended upon to produce usable water; the sewage
goes away some way, somewhere; the fire departments are good enough to keep insurance rates
within the means of the property owners; the school
buildings, always considered inadequate by the interest groups concerned with them, seem to have far
more and better laboratories and gymnasiums available for this generation than for the last. And even

[4] An address to the World Traffic Engineering Conference, Washington, D. C., Aug. 21, 1961.

when something new and unforeseen develops, as when the citizens of Los Angeles began to discover to their great surprise that fresh air could be the most precious and scarce of natural resources, the machinery of public policy moves haltingly but significantly to cope with the problem, and regulations are developed for industries and new equipment is required for automobiles. In the city of Tuscaloosa, where these lectures are delivered, it was once assumed that the pollution of the Warrior River was one of the inescapable facts of life, but now measures apparently are being taken to provide at least a degree of improvement.

When surveyors of public opinion actually go from door to door, as has been done in some of the best-financed of the metropolitan surveys, asking people what they consider to be crucial problems of metropolitan life, the answers have been surprising. Most of the people questioned were not particularly worried or unhappy about anything in their urban environment.

The facts seem to be that the great sprawling urban areas of this country fall short not so much in their achievement of the goals and ambitions of their residents, as in the degree to which they achieve or fail to achieve the speculative constructs of the intellectuals who concern themselves with the matter. The disparity is not between the metropolis as it is and the metropolis as its residents wish it; the disparity is between the existing metropolis and the City of God of the planners and the dreamers.

This is not to minimize the importance of these shortcomings. Progress in our environment comes much less often from the demands for improvement of the general population than from the vision and imagination of the few who feel that there ought to be a better way of doing something. It is the role of the intellectual to criticize the environment, as well as to describe it and to suggest ways in which it could be made better in his frame of values.

What may *we* suggest as the most significant and disturbing features of urban development and growth, with particular relation to the institutions and processes of government? What are the most important challenges in the predicament we face because our mechanisms for self-government and our ways of life are increasingly ill-adjusted? Three aspects of this predicament, or three problems if you wish, may be worth special consideration. These are: the growing homogeneity of the populations of particular areas and units; the substantial disproportions and irregularities in the patterns of public finance; and the problems of co-ordinating certain functions over large geographic areas.

When the city was a single, compact, corporate community, all its citizens, of whatever character and class, had to bring some of their affairs into the common focus and make various adjustments to each other. With a changing pattern of settlement and a breakdown of the unity of urban government, great specialization of communities and of units is now increasingly possible.

Upper-class residential suburbs can and do have a separate governmental jurisdiction and can adopt zoning rules to preserve the "character of the community." Industrial developments, outside the limits of corporate municipalities, can fend off annexation so that they will not have to pay the costs of educating the children of their workers or contend with the welfare problems of those who lose their jobs. A governmental unit with high property valuation and practically no children can exist side by side with another unit with great numbers of children to be educated and practically no property base. The central cities serve as the refuse heap for underprivileged groups and occupations which cannot escape into segregated, specialized areas. Although the central cities have many unique and important uses, although they may in some instances attract a portion of the upper class into apartment units (a circumstance which will probably become more common with the increase of two-house families) the evidence seems clear that, in housing and industrial development at least, their deteriorating properties will serve largely the marginal and less productive portions of the community from now on. The central cities act as collecting basins for the working-class migrants who cannot afford newer housing. Suburban Detroit families had a median income eleven percent above that of city dwellers in 1951; by 1959 their income was 25 percent higher.

It is easy to note the close relationship between

ethnic and class differences in our urban centers. Larger and larger proportions of the populations of the nation's central cities are becoming Negro. "Central cities of the 12 largest metropolitan areas in the United States lost 2 million white residents and gained 1 million non-white residents during the decade of the 1950's. Outside the central cities, on the other hand, 93 to 99 percent of the population in these 12 areas remained white—a proportion basically unchanged for 30 years."[5] This is certainly one of the most salient and significant facts about urban change in this country. As Morton Grodzins of the University of Chicago puts it: "Almost nothing is being done today to meet what is likely to be the nation's most pressing social problem tomorrow. The problem can be simply stated in all its bleakness: Many central cities of the great metropolitan areas of the United States are fast becoming lower class, largely Negro slums."[6] These trends seem to be accelerating, rather than approaching a limit. Harry P. Sharp indicates that in each of the twelve largest metropolitan areas the proportion of white persons began declining in the 1930's, the decline gained momentum in the 1940's, and it became pronounced in the 1950's.[7] Negroes now constitute a majority

[5] *Public Management,* XLIII (July, 1961), 163. These facts were abstracted from a paper prepared for the Population Association of America by Harry P. Sharp, director of the University of Michigan's Detroit Area Study.
[6] Morton Grodzins, *The Metropolitan Area as a Racial Problem* (Pittsburgh: University of Pittsburgh Press, 1958), p. 1.
[7] *Public Management,* XLIII, 163.

of the population of the nation's capital city, and the percentage of Negro population is very substantial in many of the older and larger cities. (It is interesting to note that in Honolulu, the only other American city with a non-white majority, this majority is rapidly being cut down. It was 84.5 percent in 1950 and only 64.3 per cent in 1960. The circumstances here, however, are greatly different from those in the continental cities.) The nine cities which in 1960 each had more than a quarter of a million non-white population are all located outside the eleven states of the Old South.

Assimilation of the Negro population will probably be much more difficult than was assimilation of earlier immigrant groups, partly because color is a more obvious distinction than national origin. Another important reason, however, is that movement out of the ghetto now will often mean movement into another governmental jurisdiction, rather than merely movement to another community within the same city.

Increasing specialization of areas, increasing homogeneity within particular units, and increasing differentiation between units have a great many public policy consequences. Governmental units with diverse economic bases and populations have very different functional needs. The town full of small new homes with many young and growing children will have tremendous needs for school construction and expansion; a high-income residential suburb may wish quality schools and a costly park and street beautification program. Older, decaying cities will have problems of police, delinquency, congestion, and welfare largely unknown to other areas. Political expression will differ greatly. Partisan political leadership seems much more effective and popular among low-income groups, new to urban life. Non-partisan elections, city manager government, and other manifestations of "good government" are much more popular in suburban areas. The old territorial areas may be involved in differences between the older personal followings of the courthouse politicians and the newer political activities of the newcomers to the unincorporated but highly urbanized fringe areas.

The splintering of the city into a diversity of jurisdictions also puts a serious strain upon the system of civic leadership. When individuals with the personal and social potential for civic leadership live in one unit, work in another, and perhaps have church or club memberships in still another, it is unlikely that they will have the concentrated interaction with others which produces the most effective and influential leadership. Moreover, with a multiplicity of memberships, both geographical and functional, the intensity of participation in any one unit is necessarily diluted. The men who run the Community Chest and Council of Social Agencies in Birmingham may live in Mountain Brook and spend much of their leisure time in a country club located in still another unit. They are not, then, first-class citizens in any one of their partial habitations.

The increasing differentiation of communities and

governmental units makes consolidation of such units difficult and places substantial obstacles in the way even of co-operative action. The antiseptic suburb wants to have no association with the corrupt politics of the central city, and the Negro leadership, pleased with its growing influence in the central city, tends to oppose any merger with the overwhelmingly white suburbs. And even though the loyalties of its residents may be divided in many ways, any governmental unit creates enough attachments and going-concern value, when reinforced by a sense of homogeneity, to resist strongly any proposals for self-destruction by merger. Furthermore, any proposed *co-operative* venture is likely to have differential impact upon particular classes. An airport seems a necessary convenience to one segment of an urban community but is placed very low on the priority list of another. The expansion of hospital facilities for the indigent is attractive to one group, not so attractive to another. The merchants of New York City would like the Port Authority to build a world trade center; the Jersey commuters would much prefer for it to take over and shore up the commuter railroads or buses. Whatever the proposed co-operative venture, there will be different reactions to it from populations of different social character, and consequent obstacles to easy agreement.

The growing segregations of urban society would not, of course, seem to be a problem to very many of its citizens. Whether by instinct or by education and long habit, most people seem initially to prefer living and working in a homogeneous community. It may be that only persistent education or long-continued and flagrant inequalities lead them to prefer integration.

A second major area of concern is the field of public finance. Just as some suggest that social and racial differences are the basic problems of the metropolitan areas, others argue that taxing and spending are the nub of the matter. As the pattern of urban life changes from one centering around a compact, corporate community to a much more diffused, far-flung arrangement, what are the changes and shifts in costs of urban services and in the resources with which to meet them?

The costs of local government services have been steadily rising, much more rapidly than personal incomes and more rapidly even than the costs of national government activities. This escalation seems certain to continue. The four major costs of state and local governments are schools, roads, welfare, and health. Public expenditures in all four fields seem likely to increase at a faster rate than population and personal income. Larger proportions of our population in the next generation will be under 21 and over 65, with corresponding increases in education and welfare costs. The increased dispersion of population and jobs adds to the part that transportation takes in total productive activity, and a large proportion of transport is paid for with public expenditures.

Continued growth of specialization of jobs and

the emphasis upon services rather than upon primary production will certainly mean increased costs to government, because a substantial proportion of those services and overhead activities are associated with specialized work and interchange. At the cutting edges of urban growth, the suburban and fringe areas, large expenditures of public investment in schools, roads, parks, and other facilities are necessary. As density decreases, public capital (and maintenance and operating as well) costs per unit of population tend to rise, up to a point. This point is reached when the density level is so low that residences and industrial and commercial establishments assume responsibility for many of their own amenities—sewage and garbage disposal, sidewalks (if any), public lighting, even water supply. To the extent that these facilities are handled through public channels, it seems apparent that more extensive land uses bring higher public capital costs.

In a provocative article Robert T. Daland presents evidence that a lower density of settlement does not necessarily produce an increased cost of public services. At the lower density, he says, some of the costs are borne by the builder or developer, instead of by the public purse. His strongest point is that the *nature* of the dispersal is a more important determinant of costs than is its degree.[8]

---

[8] Robert T. Daland, "The Impact of Urban Dispersal on Local Government Costs and Services," in Ernest A. Engelbert, *The Nature and Control of Urban Dispersal* (Berkeley and Los Angeles: University Extension, University of California, 1960), pp. 76-83.

There is no easy way to balance the differential effect of these cost patterns. Several years ago Isard and Coughlin concluded that, other things being equal, municipal costs were highest in medium-density communities, and lowest in high-density communities.[9] This conclusion was essentially founded on the inverse relationship between per unit costs and density, as modified by the self-provision of services in the lowest-density areas. Other evidence indicates that the decay and welfare costs of the central cities may be somewhat greater than the new capitalization costs of the fringes. Robert Wood made a depth analysis of 64 urban communities in the New Jersey portion of the New York metropolitan region. He concluded:

The sum and substance of the analysis seems to be this: the older cities bearing the stamps of obsolescence, high density, high industrialization, and aging inhabitants, generate higher expenses than their size alone might have led one to expect. The fact that such cities are spared some of the costs of newer communities, such as the get-going costs in opening new neighborhoods and the costs of a large school-going population, seems not to have produced a sufficient offset to the high costs associated with age and obsolescence. So the pressure for high expenditures, visible in many communities, seems to be especially pronounced in the older cities.[10]

Such generalizations must be subject to many qualifications. In some states the state pays directly

[9] Walter Isard and Robert E. Coughlin, "Municipal Costs and Revenues Resulting from Community Growth," *Journal of the American Institute of Planners* (Summer, 1956), pp. 122-141.
[10] Raymond Vernon, *Metropolis 1985* (Cambridge: Harvard University Press, 1960), pp. 172-173.

for all or most of the costs of education, but not for those of welfare; in other states welfare costs are allocated to the state governments, education costs largely to local governments. Furthermore, there are no adequate or satisfactory measures of service levels.

One of the most significant facts concerning the effect of rapid urban dispersion upon public finance, however, is this: the costs, whatever they may be, are not distributed evenly among the multiplying units of government. Some units are tax havens for industrial location, where there are neither obsolescence and welfare costs nor high costs of school construction and operation. Other units are composed of high-value residential properties, where the income per unit permits a high level of services without exorbitant rates of taxation. In still others, the costs (of either growth or decay) may be heavily concentrated. Spreading the costs out over the available resources may then be possible only by shifting them to a larger territorial jurisdiction.

There is no doubt that the urbanized sections of the country have within them the wealth and the income to meet their governmental needs.[11] Both the instruments of production and the facilities for consumption are largely located there. Whether their residents have the ingenuity to devise ways of tapping these resources may be another matter, and for the citizens of one governmental unit to devise

[11] See Harlan Cleveland, "Are the Cities Broke?" in *National Civic Review* (March, 1961), pp. 126-133.

ways and means to tap the resources located in another unit is particularly difficult.

Although Alabama and some of the other southern states constitute substantial exceptions, the property tax remains, and will probably continue to remain, the cornerstone of local finance. Its decline has been long predicted but has not yet occurred. Of the tax sources of local government income, the property tax did decline from 97 percent in 1934 to 87 percent in 1952, but there has been no further decline since that date.[12] It is true that general purpose units of government, municipalities in particular, have shifted somewhat from the property tax, but the special purpose units, particularly school districts, continue to use it almost exclusively as their source of local revenues.

Pressure to find other sources continues, partly because other sources are not so closely tied to jurisdictional boundaries, and such sources as sales or income taxes seem better adapted to matching needs with resources than are property taxes alone. Since local sales and income taxes present peculiar administrative difficulties for small units, and since they have a significantly competitive aspect among neighboring units, they seem most susceptible to use by units of considerable size or in circumstances (as in California and a few other states) where practically all of the units which might be in a competitive position are strongly motivated to use them.

[12] Briefing paper, *Local Non-Property Tax Sources,* prepared by staff members of the Advisory Commission on Intergovernmental Relations, Jan. 13, 1961, Table 1.

A third aspect of the predicament resulting from urban sprawl and splintering is that of the co-ordination of public services and functions.

Co-ordination is an abstraction which means practically nothing to the average voter and does not even mean the same thing to all sophisticated students of public affairs. It can refer to the areal co-ordination of a single service or function or to co-ordination of different functions within a single unit or area. It can mean the elimination of conflict, or the equalization of service levels, or better management with the goal of securing greater output or less input.

Although substantial disparities may exist in the level of service provided within the limits of a single governmental unit, the splintering of governmental jurisdictions certainly tends to increase these inequalities. A volunteer fire department is better than nothing, but it does not provide the same protection as does a full-time professional one. A school district with a high property evaluation per child can provide much better schools than one with a low tax base, unless the state equalization programs are especially effective. These and other inequalities of service levels produce much of the concern of people worried about the metropolitan problem.

Except in the sense that uniformity may have an aesthetic value in itself, all governmental services need not be provided equally for all people. Part of the price of securing trees and fresh air may be poor fire protection; a high degree of congestion and noise may have to be accepted in return for quicker, more convenient commuting. Although such compensations may exist, nevertheless in a divided, pluralistic local governmental arrangement many inequalities are difficult to justify or defend.

Another aspect of co-ordination of a single function or service over a large geographical area is the possibility of economy of scale. With a large unit, or with a high degree of co-ordination and co-operation between units, more specialized and productive equipment can be obtained, and it can be used more thoroughly. Special services can be provided more efficiently. A large school district can afford to have special classes and teachers for handicapped children —a service totally impractical for a small one. Machine records and accounting may provide great savings if the volume of business is sufficient to justify them.

Costs of scale may also exist in larger units because additional supervision and communication and administration are necessary. Determining the optimum size for efficient operation of any particular function or activity is very difficult, and a great many variables are certainly involved.

Even more difficult are the problems of co-ordination between different functions. The building and maintenance of roads is considered one function; the control of traffic is another; the provision of off-street parking facilities by public agencies still another; the requirement, in a zoning or a subdivision regulation, that private enterprises provide off-street parking, still another. Yet, unquestionably, all of these functions are highly interrelated. Taxing the motorist to get money for expressways so that he can drive downtown is considered highly appropriate. Yet taxing him for funds to build garages so that he can park his car after he gets downtown is frequently considered highly inappropriate. The enforcement of electrical, plumbing, construction, and sanitary codes may be regarded as one function and the operation of an urban renewal program another. Yet, if the codes are adequately enforced over a period of time, the renewal program may never be necessary.

This kind of co-ordination is difficult enough within a single governmental unit, but it is complicated immensely by the existence of several units and the location of different functions in the different units. The regulation of the rates and services of a transit corporation may be vested in a department of a city government or in an agency of the state government. The building of a new expressway, which can make or break the transit operation, may be in the hands of the state highway department and the county government. Each agency has its own constituency, its own relationship to the public, its own view of the public interest.

If the traditional model of the city existed in reality, if there were a single corporate unit, difficult problems of co-ordination would still remain. Groups and individuals differ greatly, and conditions vary in differing segments (both geographic and social) of the same community. The institutional patterns for the reconciliation of differences, for attempts at equalization, for dividing or subdividing or integrating the enterprises in an effort to secure the optimum scale, do exist in much greater degree if the community is organized as a single unit than if it is amorphous, disunited, fragmented. Adjustments and mutual accommodations and resolutions of differences do occur even in a pluralistic system of local governments, but these adjustments and co-ordinations probably come more slowly, more painfully in such circumstances.

In many respects, then, our spreading urbanized areas may be said to work remarkably well. They provide their inhabitants with a level and a variety of opportunity that is probably unprecedented. Their problems, their frictions, their difficulties are far from reaching the limits of toleration of a prosperous and affluent society. They fall short not so much of the expressed wishes of their inhabitants, as of the possibilities which outside observers would like for them to attain. But even though these areas work, and probably will continue to work, the increasing fragmentation of the social structure, the difficulties and inequities of systems of public finance, and the wasteful lack of co-ordination of many of their functions and services constitute real and significant challenges. Even if we can afford to ignore these challenges, it is socially costly and wasteful to do so.

Chapter 3

RESPONSES TO THE CHALLENGE
OF URBAN CHANGE

IF THE TRADITIONAL CITY, IN THE SENSE OF A TIGHT
corporate organization, is slowly eroding, and if this
erosion accentuates social and ethnic segregation,
emphasizes disparities and difficulties in public finance, and intensifies the problems of co-ordinating
public programs, how has thoughtful, influential
leadership responded?

The response of an individual to technological
change affecting him is ordinarily an individual response, an adjustment in his way of life. And, in
general, the response of a society is not the considered conscious response of its leadership, but the
accumulative force of all the individual responses
made by its members. This surely is the Toynbeean
response of a civilization to the challenge of its environment. Without, however, attempting to speculate at length upon the *degree* of influence wielded
by the ideals and actions of the intellectual and
political leadership of the society, we can, I hope,
accept the postulate that these leadership responses
do have considerable importance and significance.

One of the important responses, and in its long-range significance it may be the most important, has been a great quickening of research and study about urban life and urban problems.

Much of the study has revolved around specific public functions and activities. Some of it is concerned with finding solutions, or temporary alleviating arrangements, for urgent problems; some of it, while problem-oriented, is very searching in character. This type of pragmatic research is closely related to the growing specialization and professionalization of the local public service. Problems of police and fire protection, the technical problems in public health and sanitation, parks and recreation, and so on, are all being studied with greater sophistication. Extensive and highly significant research on school administration has produced, as we will note later, very important developments in arrangements for school finance and school district organization. A tremendously impressive technology is unfolding in matters of freeway location and traffic control. In Detroit, Chicago, Washington, and Philadelphia a small fraction of the federal and state funds earmarked for highway construction has been used to investigate the relationship between the patterns of land use and settlement and the needs for transportation facilities (particularly automobile transportation). Using voluminous data on present patterns of travel and of land use and alternative assumptions on future patterns, computers have been programmed to produce precise predictions on traffic needs and desires and volumes well into the future.

Another burgeoning area of study and research is in the field of city planning. Since the planners make an effort to base plans for the future upon as much data as possible concerning the present, much of their energy and effort has been devoted to collecting and analyzing information about urban life and problems. City planning agencies and staffs are growing faster than properly qualified personnel can be supplied for them. It should be noted that many of the agencies are so heavily involved with the administration of zoning and subdivision control regulations that they have very little time for study and planning. Furthermore, in their attempts to plan the urban environment, they have very considerable difficulty, just as does the society to which they belong, in reconciling their various value positions as to the nature of a good community. In spite of these handicaps, however, the city planning profession is beginning to have a significant impact, at least upon the intellectual posture of the leadership in urban areas.

A third type of research about urban public affairs is that produced by chambers of commerce, taxpayers associations, and bureaus of municipal research. Efforts by these groups to boost the economy of the area or to prevent the waste of taxpayers' money, frequently lead to serious and careful analysis of the facts, trends, and problems of the changing urban society.

Many of the welfare and health activities of large urban communities are financed by private donations rather than by tax funds. Agencies such as the Red Cross, the Salvation Army, and the Boy Scouts have multiplied and are numbered in the dozens in most metropolitan areas. They have banded together not only for fund-raising but also for better research and social planning. Most larger urban areas now have health and welfare councils, which engage in greater and lesser degrees of research, frequently focused upon social breakdown, the need for assistance, and the functioning of the health and welfare agencies. In these and other subjects, their research output is already significant and seems certain to grow.[1]

Concern about the fragmentation of local governments, or the metropolitan problem in general, has produced major surveys in most of the metropolitan communities. Many of the earlier surveys were conceived as mammoth, singleshot efforts to arrive at a "solution" of the problems of the government of metropolitan areas, and they proposed ambitious plans of governmental reorganization which were practically never acceptable to the leadership or citizenry of the communities studied. "Metropology," as Charles Adrian has called it,[2] has taken different and somewhat more sophisticated approaches in re-

[1] See *Issues in Community Welfare Research* (Indianapolis: Health and Welfare Council of Indianapolis and Marion County and United Community Funds and Councils of America, 1958).
[2] In *Public Administration Review,* XXI (Summer, 1961), 148.

cent years. Some of the more recent surveys have been made from the perspective of the state government and have been devoted to investigating the impact of state legislation and policy upon urban development throughout the state. From these studies have come policy recommendations concerning modification in state legislation which may permit and facilitate certain types of urban governmental developments without imposing any immediate reorganization. Other surveys, focused locally, have been oriented less to problem and reform than were their predecessors and more to analysis of the attitudes and needs of the individual residents of the urban complex.

These metropolitan surveys have sometimes been financed by the existing governmental machinery, or by parts of it, but they have seldom had the enthusiastic support and participation of the existing political leadership. Sponsored and promoted by the economic and social "notables"—the segments of the population to whom community leadership would be attributed by many supposedly knowledgeable citizens—they have involved the practicing politicians in much smaller measure. Economic and social leaders have become concerned about both the reputed and the real problems resulting from changes in the shape and composition of their environment, and have hoped to find some salvation through bringing in experts to prescribe for the ailments they see and think they see.

The attitude of incumbent political officials and

active political leadership toward such surveys has
been equivocal. Sometimes they have been confronted with particular problems to which they saw
no easy, viable, and at the same time acceptable,
solution, and have had some real hopes that a survey
might bring to light a path never before perceptible
to them. Occasionally they have used the survey as
a device to stall off uncomfortable pressures for a
period. In many public policy areas research is frequently used as a substitute for action. In nearly
every instance, however, the professional politicians
have been somewhat skeptical of the possibilities of
producing revolutionary changes in local government through the medium of survey and recommen-
dation.

Some instances of attempts at particularly broad,
long-range community research have been aided and
in considerable measure stimulated by support from
philanthropic foundations. In Kansas City, Dayton,
Detroit, Philadelphia, and Washington, institutional
arrangements have been formed to carry on continuing basic research about the nature and changes
of the urban environment. Considering the number
of phenomena and variables available for investiga-
tion, however, even these enterprises, substantially
financed in comparison to most public affairs research projects, have tremendous problems of selec-
tion and focus.

The academic world has certainly occupied its
appropriate role in the intellectual vanguard of this
evolving research on urban life. Among the es-

tablished social science disciplines, sociology, geography, and political science have a very substantial background of accumulated learning about the urban aspects of their fields of inquiry, and all have had new surges of life and interest in urban affairs in recent years. Particularly noteworthy is the growth of interest in the field of urban economics, a development which is substantially broader and deeper than the rather limited older concern of the discipline with land and real estate economics. Some large-scale and impressive studies of specific urban communities from an economic standpoint have been made recently, including an especially important one on New York, the largest urban center in this hemisphere.

The first steps have been taken toward getting the federal government and its financial resources involved in research about urban affairs. For some years the federal housing acts have provided small funds to support research about housing, and the federal government has been subsidizing city planning activities for small cities and for metropolitan areas for several years. Each new federal housing act has increased the amount of this support and expanded the specifications. Although federal appropriations for agricultural research are many times larger than those for urban-related research activities, the camel's nose is under the tent, and it is reasonable to predict that more of the camel will follow.

In addition to study and research, what other response has been made by those beginning to perceive the significant changes in urban public life? Aside from the nation-state itself, the city has been the most distinct and operational community around which a unit of self-government could be fashioned. As the identity of this community and unit has tended to fade and blur, there has been, perhaps understandably, considerable floundering and diversity in the responses of urban intellectual leaders. It may be useful to suggest, in over-simplified form, three different types of response, three different kinds of bias or general emotional reactions, to the growingly explosive urban development.

One response has been to try to use all of the forces of public policy to restore the disappearing community. A second response has been to try to find the urban community again in suburbia. Still a third has been to seek it anew in Metro.

William H. Whyte, Jr., one of the editors of *Fortune,* began the introduction to a very perceptive volume, *The Exploding Metropolis,* with the sentence: "This is a book by people who like cities." And as the subtitle to the volume the editors put this: "A study of the assault on urbanism and how our cities can resist it." One response to urban dispersal, then, is to use the tools and weapons of planning and the powers of the state insofar as possible to check and slow the process, to bring back the residents who left the corporate community, and to introduce those who are moving into it in such a way that they will become involved participants in the city and its affairs. Those who react in this way would like renewal of the decaying sections of the city on massive scales, and an establishment of a new quality of urbanity-cum-amenity. They would like to renovate and subsidize mass transit, and do everything feasible to discourage the advance of the automobile revolution and to encourage sufficient concentration of the populations to provide, again, a definable corporate community for the city. Confronted with an exploding metropolis, they would like to man the defenses and contain the tide within reinforced and reinvigorated cities. Mrs. Jacobs, in her book, takes a stand in favor of this response, though she deplores the nature of some of the recommended renewal enterprises.

A second major response to the withering away of the city is the attempt to find it anew in suburbia. In Robert Wood's book, *Suburbia,* the author says in a section he calls "The Case for the Reappearing Community":

The challenge the suburban community confronts is the immense scale of industrialization and urbanization of modern life. The response is a sorting out of the disparate, disruptive factors which modern specialization has produced and a reassembling of them in manageable clusters. Out of the great urban mass of occupations, classes, technical skills, income levels, races and creeds, particular variants seem to be coalescing into smaller units with definite conscious identity. This isolation, in the suburbs, of certain types of metropolitan people into groups is creating a new kind of homogeneity, participation, and equality.[3]

[3] Robert C. Wood, *Suburbia* (Boston: Houghton Mifflin Co., 1959), p. 105.

With some differences in their evaluation of homogeneity as a desirable characteristic of the new
suburban corporate entities, this is the prevailing
response of the British planners, expressed best in
the new towns program. They propose strong positive efforts to stimulate and encourage dispersal, but
they insist particularly on grouping the dispersed
population into tight new corporate communities of
small and manageable size.

A third response, the search for a new community
of metropolitan dimensions, has certainly been the
most common response of American intellectual
leadership. Recognizing that growth and spreading
of the urban areas is inevitable, these people argue
that there is still a distinguishable and discoverable
community unit; that, while the edges may be fuzzy,
an urban community of Greater Birmingham, or
Greater Indianapolis, or Greater Miami may be
accurately and properly discerned. What is needed,
then, is just the shaping of governmental institutions
to fit the realities of the community. The concept
of a corporate governmental unit, performing services for its residents, is still pertinent and applicable;
we need only to reshape the governmental structure
to eliminate or at least minimize the splintering and
fractionation and to vest in a new metropolitan government the power to govern. This philosophy has
dominated most of the metropolitan government surveys of the last half generation. For example, the
report of the survey of metropolitan Birmingham
published by the Bureau of Public Administration of

the University of Alabama in 1949 suggests that absence of community-wide civic spirit, a lack of unified planning, inadequate tax basis, and neglect of vital functions due to the existence of competing units have made it difficult if not impossible to obtain the coordinate action necessary to meet governmental responsibilities that are no longer local but metropolitan in character. The opportunity is afforded the citizens of the Birmingham Metropolitan District to check the present drift in that direction and to take positive steps to support the trends toward unified governmental action.[4]

And the report ends by expressing the hope that "the aspiration of Greater Birmingham be realized in the creation of Metropolitan Birmingham."[5]

Although the rationale for the rediscovery of an enlarged, single urban community has been accepted by the leadership of a good many cities, it has been exceedingly difficult to sell to the electorate. In Birmingham the commission of distinguished citizens appointed to study the matter approved the various proposals for consolidation by votes ranging from 19 to 3 to 22 to 0, but the voters of both the state of Alabama and Jefferson County turned down the enabling constitutional amendments by substantial majorities. Similar proposals in dozens of American cities have been quietly laid to rest by a political leadership which was not convinced of their acceptability, or have been defeated, often resoundingly, by the voters at the polls.

[4] Weldon Cooper, *Metropolitan County* (University, Alabama: Bureau of Public Administration, 1949), p. 134.
[5] *Ibid.*, p. 145.

Only in Miami, in this country, has a major, general purpose, new metropolitan government been created. (Another has very recently been approved in Nashville.) In Miami, where the old separate units were allowed to remain, the division of powers between these units and the new metropolitan government is confusing even to lawyers and largely beyond the comprehension of the average citizens. Much of the continued urbanization of the region is occurring outside the limits of even the new unit, and continuing strong efforts are made to scuttle the new charter.

Although attempts to return to the corporate central city, to find viable suburban units, and especially to promote a new metropolitan-wide community represent three types of response to current challenges, most thoughtful observers do not rely completely upon such over-simplified approaches. While disagreements and differences and many varieties of opinion are found among students of local government, and various kinds of reform and reorganization of local government patterns are advocated, the goals and value assumptions, the basic political instrumentalities and institutional arrangements favored have a great deal in common. It will further our thinking, perhaps, if we take the time to inspect some of these basic value assumptions and the chief means commonly urged for achieving these values. Then we can look briefly at some of the basic political obstacles to quick achievement of these "reforms."

First, what are the value goals suggested as basic in the thinking of most students of local government in this country in this generation—or at least that portion of those students willing to confess to having any value position, or in whose writings or discussions a value position may be said to be implicit? I do not suggest that these are the absolutely basic, or ultimate values; it may be that any so-called "value" is merely the instrument for the achievement of some other, more basic goal. Without pushing this qualification further, however, I do suggest that a few fundamental value assumptions tend to guide the proposals of most current proponents of governmental change at the local level. In earlier lectures in this same series, Emmette Redford described a set of "ideals" for public administration in general.[6] Some similarities, and some differences, between his list and mine may be noted.

1. *Responsiveness.* The most generally accepted goal of a set of governmental arrangements in a democratic society apparently is responsiveness to the wishes of the people. Procedures and arrangements which facilitate the expression of the popular will, such as opportunities for public discussion and association, are usually regarded as necessary means for the achievement of this goal. (Those who think that the people are mistaken—and many intellectuals

---

[6] Emmette S. Redford, *Ideal and Practice in Public Administration* (University, Alabama: University of Alabama Press, 1958). Another published set of goals, one postulated peculiarly for local government and one with which I was associated, may be found in Arthur Maass (ed.), *Area and Power* (Glencoe, Ill.: The Free Press, 1959).

and leaders frequently think this—put their trust in education; hopefully, the people will change their mind when sufficiently educated or informed.) This statement of a goal, however, begs the question of the size or character of the units of people whose wishes are to be carried out.

2. *Equity*. The second basic goal or value is equity, which involves equal treatment for persons equally situated and insists that classification or differential treatment is acceptable only when based upon rational grounds. To distribute the burdens or the benefits of governmental programs unevenly stirs up the sense of injustice.

3. *The Public Welfare*. Many prefer other definitions for this vague phrase, but I use it here to mean an open-ended collection of common or widely-shared personal values and wants—health, safety, material income, knowledge, beauty, and the like. While wide philosophical differences may appear in the definition and boundaries of these ends, certainly in practice a tremendous area of agreement concerning their desirability obtains.

4. *Community*. In some measure community is merely a desirable or even essential element of the public welfare. Only to the degree that there is a sharing, a community, of *personal* values and goals can there be a *public* welfare. In another sense, however, social cohesion, as contrasted to social divisiveness, is a value goal in itself.

5. *Efficiency*. Clearly subordinate, not a primary end in itself, nevertheless efficiency is so im-

portant and so pervasive that it deserves listing in this company. It is a simple concept, in either engineering or social policy. It is the ratio between output and input—output in terms of the basic goals or ends and input in terms of money, or man-hours, or blood, sweat, and tears. The outputs are to be maximized, the inputs minimized. Difficult as it is to define and measure the units of output and input, the goal is always and inescapably present.

6. *Orderliness.* Although it is rarely included in such a listing as this, and is difficult to defend on the same level, there can be little doubt that order and symmetry have frequently been the governing values of proponents of governmental reform.

These goals or ends—responsiveness, equity, public welfare, community, efficiency, and orderliness —have been the chief aims of the leaders of American urban communities as they tried to adapt their institutions to developments in the environment. With such values to provide the guidelines for the responses to urban growth and change, what are some of the chief institutional and process arrangements which will furnish the greatest opportunity to attain the goals? What constitutional policies have been generally or frequently advocated as standards for urban local government in the current world? Without any pretense of being exhaustive, several very important ones may be listed:

1. *Home rule.* If government is to be responsive to the people, it follows that any group or unit of people must be allowed to decide as much of its own

destiny as can be made consistent with a similar privilege on the part of others. But in practice this principle of self-determination has very great difficulties. Where is "home"? To me, home is the United States, or Indiana, or Monroe County, or Bloomington, or Perry Township, or the fifteenth precinct, or even my own household. Sovereignty or complete self-determination in one of these homes is inconsistent with the same attribute in another. The application of the principle of home rule to a confused jumble of governments in a metropolitan area is practically impossible.

2. *Political responsibility.* Adherence to the principle that governmental agents and policies should be responsible to the will of the voters takes many forms, but the application of these forms is often difficult and even inconsistent. One aspect of the attachment to political responsibility is the assumption that basic matters should be settled by referendum. But how basic should a matter be before being settled in this way?

Also associated with the concept of political responsibility, and with the basic goal of equity, is the principle of "one man, one vote," or the goal of, at the minimum, a *wide* distribution of political power and influence. Since identification and measurement of political influence is far from easy, substantial differences of opinion prevail as to how much it is distributed or concentrated in American cities at present.[7] How the reorganization of units

[7] There is a large and growing body of literature concerned with com-

would affect political influence has received speculation, but little else, although in some cities—Cleveland seems a clear case—the distribution of political representation has been close to the center of controversies concerning reorganization.

The principle of political responsibility sometimes leads to advocating direct responsibility to the electorate for a particular function, such as schools; sometimes it means advocating a single line of general responsibility for all governmental functions, rather than separate lines of responsibility for separate functions.

3. *A preference for larger units.* It is frequently argued that a more satisfactory attainment of the public welfare, a greater degree of equity in the sharing of the burdens and benefits of public programs, and even a higher degree of responsiveness can be achieved in a governmental unit which is as big as possible. Of course, if the principle of home rule is applied to the smaller units, and if the principle of political responsibility is followed either through referenda or through the behavior of politicians sensitive to the wishes of the electorate, the achievement of this standard turns out to be completely inconsistent with the ones previously suggested.

4. *General purpose governments.* Paul Ylvisaker said in his "criteria for a 'proper' areal division of

---

munity power structure. Some of the most interesting analysis, and some evidence on the matter, are in Robert Dahl, *Who Governs* (New Haven: Yale University Press, 1961).

powers" that "the assignment of powers to component areas should in each case be a general one, covering the whole range of governmental functions, rather than a partial one related only to particular functions."[8] He and others argue that both efficient attainment of the common values, which I have called the public welfare, and the effective achievement of real responsiveness to the public will can be more adequately achieved through multi-functional units than through single-function ones.

5. *Executive leadership.* Within a particular governmental unit, the most effective focus for political responsibility and the institutional center for the guidance and direction of vigorous programs of public policy seem to many to be in the executive branch, particularly in a strong single chief executive. For more than fifty years, developments in national and state governments as well as in local governments have led to more reliance upon executive leadership, and many observers are convinced that there is high correlation between the presence of executive leadership within a governmental unit and the effectiveness of the particular unit in achieving some of the more basic goals suggested earlier. Herbert Kaufman, in an article entitled "Emerging Conflicts in the Doctrines of Public Administration,"[9] suggested that the newest governing doctrine of students of public administration was "the quest for executive leadership." The other two

[8] In Maass (ed.), p. 34.
[9] *American Political Science Review,* L (Dec., 1956), 1057-1073.

"core values" which he described were "the quest for representativeness" and "the quest for neutral competence." These correspond substantially to some of the basic *means* or *tools* for goal achievement outlined here. Kaufman argued that the three quests had sometimes reinforced each other and had sometimes come in conflict.

6. *Administrative integration.* This involves grouping various administrative functions of a governmental unit into a single institutional pattern, subject to a single control center through a hierarchical arrangement. While such an arrangement may have been impelled in part by the aesthetic attractiveness of order and symmetry, other justifications are commonly advanced. Some time ago, writing about state administration (and the justifications are comparable) I said: "Two basic arguments for administrative integration are apparent and these are closely related. The first of the arguments is the desirability of coordinating state administrative activities. ... the other basic argument for integration is that responsibility to the people is furthered if there is a single focus for the whole governmental program."[10]

7. *Professionalization of public service.* The development of specialization and expertise seems regularly to have accompanied technological improvement in nearly every field, and the public service is certainly no exception. It has seemed both

[10] York Willbern, "Administration in State Governments," *The Forty-Eight States* (New York: The American Assembly, 1955), pp. 119-120.

inevitable and highly desirable. There is little doubt about the contribution of professionalization to the efficiency of government and to the furtherance of the goals associated with the public welfare. But considerable doubt prevails as to the degree to which it has enhanced responsiveness.

These, then, are some of the more important, basic values or goals of local self-government and some of the principles or standards of public institutions considered most likely to achieve these goals. To gain responsiveness, equity, public welfare, community, efficiency, and orderliness in our patterns of local government, the intellectual leadership of our urban areas has favored home rule, political responsibility, larger units, general purpose government, executive leadership, administrative integration, and professionalization. While most or all of these have been questioned from time to time by skeptics and by heretics, they have been generally and widely accepted by academic students and writers, by the adherents of the National Municipal League and the League of Women Voters, and even, rather commonly, by the chambers of commerce and taxpayers associations and the economic, journalistic and social notables of the urban communities.

To some, such goals and standards are thought to be myths, in the sense of intuitively accepted symbols which provide motivation. Others would argue that the goals are inherently desirable and attractive and that the relationship between the goals and the doctrines is based upon enough evidence, or upon plausible enough reasoning, to constitute as sound a body of theory as can be expected as a basis for social action in this highly complicated and imperfect world. At any rate, these doctrines and principles define and bound in considerable measure the responses which the intellectual community has advocated for the challenge of urban change. To some extent they represent efforts to hold fast to the institutions of the past, regardless of social change. Much more often, they have guided efforts for substantial change in governmental institutions, with the hope that these institutions will then be better adapted to the emerging patterns of urban life.

The achievement of these goals, the effectuation of these governmental doctrines, has not been easy. The same thing could be said of many of them that has been said of Christianity: it is not that it has been tried and found wanting, but rather that it has been found hard and not tried.

One of the great difficulties has been that the goals themselves may not always be consistent with each other. Certainly some of the means and instruments run afoul of each other and it is often possible to maximize one only at substantial cost to another.

Assuming, however, that theory can develop some reconciliation among the goals and institutional arrangements, some very important aspect of political reality, or what appears to be political reality, has frequently blocked the adoption of part or all of the reform programs. Some of the most important of these political obstacles may be noted.

1. *Resistance to change.* The structure of any

continuing social institution is likely to offer considerable impediment to innovation and change. Local government arrangements in this country are certainly not an exception. The institutional arrangements for the machinery and processes of public decision-making are considered in our system to be constitutional in character, and ordinarily constitutional changes are much more difficult of accomplishment than are changes in substantive policy. Slow as are the changes in the social order of our urban communities, constitutional changes in the political order are slower still.

2. *Heavier weighting to veto powers.* Although the political system of a local area or community is not formally arranged like the Security Council in the United Nations, many segments of the community have what amounts to the power of veto. In general, positive action is taken only when there is a substantial degree of consensus; when, as is frequently the case, several different governmental units are involved in a matter, consensus may even be legally and structurally necessary. Even within a single unit, a clear dissent by a significant minority may oftentimes be sufficient to block an innovation. Any one of a group of centers of power will be able, usually, to exercise its influence much more successfully and effectively in a negative direction than in a positive one.

3. *The existence of vested interests.* The distribution of benefits from governmental programs in effect at any one time gives some individuals and

groups advantages which they would lose in a re-shuffling. Even though there might be some total gain in progress toward desired goals, some groups would suffer losses and deprivations. These vested interests, of course, would be defended strongly.

4. *Non-rational behavior of political participants.* No matter what the goals or interests may be, neither an individual nor a group can be expected always to seek them rationally. The facts are never fully known; the evidence as to the consequences of a particular action may be ignored; inaccurate assessments and calculations of a situation are frequent.

Urban intellectual leaders may agree, at least in part, on the goals of local public affairs and even on the general outlines of institutional action needed to achieve them, but governmental adaptation to technological and social change has come very slowly. Partly because these goals and actions are not always mutually consistent, partly for the reasons just outlined, our responses to our urban challenges have often been weak, irresolute, and confused.

In a society as diverse and varied as ours, consistent and clear-cut responses would be too much to expect, even from leaders and the intellectual community. Certainly, increasing attention is being given to these changes. Research, study, and speculation are growing apace. In terms of public policy and institutions, simple and orderly responses have not succeeded. We can restore neither the rural life of our grandfathers nor the tight, compact corporate cities of some of our fathers, nor have we been very successful in finding new arrangements for community either in suburbia or in the metropolis. We can and are giving serious consideration to the goals in our arrangements for managing our local affairs and to the instruments and devices which we think may best help us attain these goals. Neither the goals nor the instruments are, however, completely consistent with each other, and very significant obstacles must be surmounted before some of the desirable devices are adopted.

Chapter 4

CREEPING TRANSITIONS IN LOCAL GOVERNMENT

IN SPITE OF STRUCTURAL RESISTANCES, AND VETO powers, and vested interests, and irrationalities, governmental institutions do change, and they change in response to the forces of transitions in social ecology. The changes may not come as a conscious response to challenge, and they may occur in unexpected and deviant fashion, but governmental institutions adapt themselves to social forces and social needs. And it is comforting to think, although it might not be easy to demonstrate, that these adjustments and adaptations come somewhat more easily in an open, fluid society such as ours than in others of a different character.

It may be that the student and reformer of local government will find it more rewarding to examine trends in government's adaptation to changing urban patterns and to predict and try to guide some of these trends, than it has been to try to create grand and sweeping designs and then promote them.

Cities are very, very far from being dead, although

some forces have tended to damage the tightness and utility of their corporate communities. They have the solid historical footing of being considered *the* appropriate unit through which people living in proximity with each other could join together for their common government. The powers, the responsibilities, the institutional machinery, the sense of civic responsibility, which have been accumulated out of this historic posture, cannot be quickly and easily eroded. Legal powers of cities, while limited, are ordinarily far more extensive than are those of general territorial units or of special districts. Even though the political leadership of the central cities may be formally responsible to only a segment of the urban electorate, it is still identified, and identifies itself, as the chief focal point of urban community efforts. Edward Banfield and Robert Dahl have published intensive studies of the structure and workings of political power and influence in Chicago and New Haven; different as the two urban areas are, the central character in each account is clearly the mayor.

Perhaps even more important, cities, both central and suburban, have developed administrative machinery which makes it possible for them to attack some of the problems of urban life with far more vigor and effect than can the general territorial units, most of the special districts, or, in many cases, even the state itself. In spite of rumors and realities of corruption, the city police forces are systematic, at least semi-professional, and reasonably efficient; the fire departments are not amateurish; the public works and traffic control agencies get their jobs done; and the city council and mayor or manager provide a clear focus of political decision-making, exposed and reasonably responsive to public pressures, which is frequently absent in any other unit of government active in local affairs.

These accumulated institutional and political assets have tremendous weight in spite of the demographic forces which tend to cripple the viability of the city as a corporate community. They may continue partly because of social lag, and they may be diminishing in strength, but their influence will be very great for a long time.

One of the significant creeping trends in local government, one which has been occurring with little notice for a long time, is that the legal corporate limits of a city are less and less significant as a real boundary for its services and control. Since a city has a central position in relation to an urbanizing hinterland, and since administrative and political machinery has been developed for its use, more and more activities ignore the "walls of the city" concept. Even though the only official "members," or citizens, of a city are those who reside within its limits, its activities have a great impact on persons outside.

Many of the services and functions conducted within city limits serve a much wider group of constituents or customers. The civic auditoriums, the city parks and recreational facilities, the city libraries, some urban educational institutions, certainly have this outreach. The city is responsible for much of the transportation network extending through an entire region. The city is intimately linked with the public transit service, sometimes through ownership and operation, more often through intimate association and control. Bus and railroad terminals are promoted and assisted by the city. Airports are still, for the most part, built and operated by central cities, despite a strong tendency to seek aid from larger governmental units. Cities frequently operate the public hospitals and are often vitally involved in the public health and inspection activities, which protect larger regions.

In addition many of the city's activities are actually conducted outside the corporate limits. In Alabama, the concept of the "police jurisdiction" provides an institutional base for these activities much stronger than is common elsewhere, but there are similar operations in many other states. Extraterritorial planning, zoning, and subdivision control are now common. Extending municipal public utility services beyond city limits is almost standard; in fact, in some states, the legislature has declared that a central city may not refuse such services. Through contractual relationships such basics as fire protection and police patroling are frequently extended outside corporate limits, either to other governmental units or to private groups or individuals.

These developments which are expected to continue and to grow prove that the city itself is not withering away; rather, the city is changing in nature and character. Instead of a tight corporate community providing definite services and functions for its own membership, the city is now a somewhat fuzzy and indefinite association, supplying a mixed and indeterminate range of services to an amorphous and indeterminate constituency.

The boundaries of cities are much less rigid in some states than in others. In a few states, boundaries of cities are still shifted rather easily to adjust to the patterns of urban growth and settlement. But this is not the usual rule.

It is generally true that it has been impossible to encompass the spreading wave of urban growth and development within the legal limits of the central cities. Central cities in metropolitan areas increased their population by only 5.6 million, or 10.7 percent, during the 1950-1960 decade, while the portions of metropolitan areas outside the central cities grew 17.9 million, or 48.6 percent. Almost all of the population growth of the central cities of metropolitan areas has been through annexation. In terms of their 1950 boundaries, the central cities of the nation's metropolitan areas "showed a population rise of only 767,000 or 1.5 percent during the 1950-1960 decade."[1] The remainder of their population increase, 4.1 million, came through annexation of portions of the area which had previously been in the fringe.

In the big, old cities where annexation has almost

[1] Advisory Commission on Intergovernmental Relations, *Governmental Structure, Organization, and Planning in Metropolitan Areas* (Washington: U. S. Government Printing Office, 1961), p. 6.

completely stopped, the central cities have uniformly
lost rather than gained population. In these areas,
the pattern of governmental boundaries seems to
have substantially crystallized, the fringes have arranged alternative ways of securing urban services,
and significant annexation to the central city is no
longer considered feasible. In some sections of the
country, however, this crystallization has not occurred. Of the 212 Standard Metropolitan Statistical
Areas, the central cities in 65 *increased* their proportion of the population between 1950 and 1960. In
these areas the central city grew more rapidly than
did the fringe and increased its position of domi-
nance. These proportionately greater central city
increases mean either massive annexation or pre-
vious inclusion within urban boundaries of great
areas of undeveloped land; in any case, the effect
is approximately the same—the spreading populations are kept within the city corporate community,
rather than spilling out over the external countryside.

In view of the general trends already noted, it
is obvious that these 65 central cities constitute exceptions to the general rule, both in numbers and
in proportionate size. Furthermore, it is interesting
to note that they tend to be concentrated in a few
sections of the country.

In each of twelve states, located in three separate
but contiguous regions of the country, the central
cities of a majority of the metropolitan areas increased population at a more rapid rate than did the

fringes. (The census definition is used in each instance; there can be a good many arguments about the application of these definitions, but some agreed-upon standard must be used, and this is certainly the best known.) The first region includes South Dakota, North Dakota, and Montana, where in all four of the metropolitan areas the central cities increased their proportion of the metropolitan population. Arizona, New Mexico, Texas, and Oklahoma comprise the second region, and here in 25 of the 27 metropolitan areas the central cities grew more rapidly than the fringe. And in the third region, which includes Mississippi, Alabama, Georgia, North Carolina, and Virginia, the central city's population increased faster than that of the fringe in 17 of the 24 metropolitan areas. Nineteen of the 65 central cities which increased their percentage are located in the state of Texas.

What may be said about these particular regions? Most significantly, perhaps, they contain states in which the urbanizing forces, both centrifugal and centripetal, while powerful, seem comparatively new. These are not the old urban centers. The urban growth here has been so new and so rapid that patterns for providing urban services to fringe areas are still flexible and no rigid barriers prevent the existing central cities—the only really effective source—from extending the span of such services. While Boston, Buffalo, Milwaukee, and St. Louis are hemmed in by what Frank P. Zeidler, former Mayor of Milwaukee, called the "iron ring" of suburbs, Tucson, Oklahoma City, Mobile, and even Savannah were able to increase their land areas by 600 percent, 500 percent, 500 percent, and 200 percent, respectively.[2] As the phrase "newly-emerging" is frequently applied to certain countries in the world to avoid calling them "underdeveloped," perhaps the phrase "newly-urbanizing" can be applied to some of these states. While California and Florida may also be newly-urbanizing, the growths there have been so massive and so sweeping that extending central city limits has not been an effective device. Other factors also help to explain the greater degree of annexation in some of these states. In some of the southern states where the property tax is much smaller, so that by annexation unincorporated areas can receive additional services at little additional cost, there is much less resistance by the fringe.

While the most prominent users of annexation have been some of these newly-urbanizing states, it is receiving new attention in many areas. The applicable statutes have generally given very high priority to the principle of self-determination of groups to be annexed. Generally, the group to be annexed must take the initiative, and almost always their consent must be obtained by referendum. Where these principles have been modified, very substantial annexations are occurring. In Texas, for example, where, in 19 of 21 metropolitan areas, central cities increased their proportion of the metropolitan population, cities are permitted to put pro-

[2] *Ibid.*, p. 64.

visions into their home-rule charters authorizing them to expand their limits without the consent of the annexed populations, if they are not already resident in an incorporated city. Really massive annexations in Texas have resulted—even the large cities of Houston, Dallas, and San Antonio more than doubled their land area between 1950 and 1960. Virginia has long had a provision for determination by judicial inquiry, rather than by referendum; North Carolina adopted a somewhat similar provision in 1959. The Advisory Commission on Intergovernmental Relations, which includes members from cities, counties, states, and the federal government, using the appropriately cautious words of a large group with differing constituencies, recently recommended:

that the states examine critically their present constitutional and statutory provisions governing annexation of territory to municipalities, and that they act promptly to eliminate or amend—at least with regard to metropolitan areas—provisions that now hamper the orderly and equitable extension of municipal boundaries so as to embrace unincorporated territory in which urban development is under way or in prospect. As a minimum, authority to initiate annexation proceedings should not rest solely with the area or residents desiring annexation, but should also be available to city governing bodies. There is also merit to the proposition that the inhabitants of minor outlying unincorporated territory should not possess an absolute power to veto a proposed annexation which meets appropriate standards of equity.[3]

Annexation, as a method of enlarging the urban

[3] *Ibid.*, p. 21.

community more or less continually to accommodate population spread, is probably not feasible in older urban areas, and may fall short generally as the dispersal tendencies become even stronger; but certainly some cities are running a good race in their efforts to extend their limits as fast as the urban population inundates the countryside.

Partial adjustment to urban sprawl by decreasing the importance of corporate boundaries, and vigorous but spotty efforts to include larger portions of the urbanizing area, are significant, and may be expected to continue. Another modification of the historic model is the growing tendency to limit and control strictly the privilege of incorporation. Traditionally, cities, or villages, or towns, have become legal units voluntarily when an appropriate number of interested citizens residing in an area not already included in an incorporated community demonstrated through required procedures that residents and property holders consented. Now that urbanization resembles a thin veneer spread over wide areas and identifiable compact communities are much less apparent, the process of incorporation takes on a somewhat different meaning. Some incorporations occur to prevent the extension of extraterritorial control by an adjacent municipality. In those states where annexation can occur without full consent of those being annexed, some occur to prevent annexation. In other instances incorporations are made for extremely limited purposes, and the new corporation relies upon adjacent cities or upon general territorial units for a wide range of the services which it would ordinarily supply for itself. Incorporation is sometimes stimulated by tax-sharing programs of the state or some program of grants-in-aid.

While such suburban incorporations continue, and make ever more complex and pluralistic the patterns of governmental units, significant movements are taking place to limit drastically such privileges. In a good many states, when a particular urbanized area becomes sufficiently cluttered with corporate communities, further incorporation in the area has been forbidden by the state, with the hope of concentrating responsibility for urban services upon the extraterritorial activities of existing cities, or, more frequently, upon the general purpose territorial units. Some other states are forbidding new incorporations adjacent to or nearby large existing cities or setting the minimum standards of population, or population density, much higher in such urbanized environment. Other states provide for review, either administrative or judicial, of the necessity and desirability of the new incorporation. The Advisory Commission on Intergovernmental Relations recommended "rigorous statutory standards for the establishment of new municipal incorporations within the geographic boundaries of metropolitan areas" and "administrative review and approval of such proposed new incorporation."[4]

4 *Ibid.,* p. 39.

These growing limitations upon the freedom to incorporate are intended to restrain continued multiplication of units which constitute segments only of larger urban complexes, and to achieve one or more of the following purposes: (1) strengthen the extraterritorial activities of existing municipalities, (2) make annexation to existing units easier and more likely, and (3) encourage the provision of urban services by general territorial units.

Just as significant as the adjustments and modifications of the corporate units are the gradual changes reshaping the territorial units in urbanizing areas.

First, a few comments about townships. Generally speaking, territorial towns or townships were created only in New England, the Middle Atlantic states, and the Middle West. In the Middle West, where, in spite of large and growing urban areas, most land area is still overwhelmingly rural, the townships have been dying on the vine because improved transportation and communication make it possible for the counties to take over most of the functions of territorial government. In Indiana townships were relieved of their responsibility for rural roads in 1931; townships continue to have some limited general assistance functions in the field of public welfare, but most public welfare activities were vested in the county in the middle 1930's; and the state is currently engaged in a statewide school reorganization which will transfer township school functions from all but the most urban townships. While they may linger legally for a long while, townships will eventually have practically no significant governmental functions. In New England where the distinction between corporate and territorial units was never clear, the towns are becoming more and more like urban units of government, eliminating the necessity for municipal incorporations in many places and, in some states, avoiding also any significant role for the counties. In Connecticut county governments were recently officially abolished, and in Rhode Island they have had practically no significance. In some of the Middle Atlantic states, the towns or townships are playing a very ambivalent role. In the rural areas they are being eclipsed by the county, but in many of the metropolitan areas, urban functions are being thrust upon them because of the need for various kinds of activities which are not being adequately conducted elsewhere.

While the urban role of townships may have a doubtful future, largely because even in areas of congested settlement they ordinarily encompass only a minor fraction of any particular urbanized region, the counties are in a very different position. With few exceptions, all the land area and all the citizens in the United States are within the jurisdiction of county governments, and county governments do not overlap each other. The tide of metropolitanism has spread beyond county boundaries in many instances, but the Census Bureau says that 133 of the nation's 212 metropolitan areas are encompassed within the boundaries of a single county. Even in instances like Chicago, Los Angeles, and Detroit,

where more than one county is included in the defined metropolitan area, a single county is commonly
far larger and more comprehensive, in both area
and population, than is the central city.

In every area of substantial population, with perhaps a few exceptions in New England, county
governments are rapidly becoming functionally urbanized. At the very heart of the transformation in
patterns of urban life is the building, maintenance,
and operation of roads, traditionally the biggest
single activity of county government, and second
only to education as a function of local government
in general. Today, the county road becomes a street,
often with curb and gutter, with street signs and
traffic lights, and a traffic engineer and traffic police are needed. The width of right-of-way and width
of paving become weighty problems. Drainage structures are of critical importance; when a new subdivision, with rooftops and streets and driveways and
sidewalks and lawns, replaces farm or woodland, the
runoff of water doubles and triples and quadruples.
Professional engineering, rather than guessing at the
lay of the land, becomes imperative. In the more
thickly-populated areas, the county may need to get
into the business of freeways and cloverleaf inter-
sections.

Other traditional county functions are also transformed. The sheriff's deputies put on uniforms and
operate regular patrols with radio communication
and perhaps even install a fingerprint laboratory.
Instead of the old poor farm, many an urban county

must now operate a general charity hospital, serving the needs of all the residents of all the county, and in addition a big professional welfare department. Not only are old functions transformed; new functions come thrusting in. Since public health problems —inspections of dairies and restaurants and water supplies—can hardly be confined within corporate limits, part or all of the public health responsibilities may be shifted from the city to the county. In order to get the benefit of a larger tax base, many of the regular municipal activities may be similarly shifted —the support of an airport, or of an auditorium, or of a public library.

The ways in which these transformed and enlarged functions are administered constitute interesting examples of the processes of institutional innovation and adaptation. Certainly the traditional machinery of county government has been little adapted to the performance of the complex, difficult, specialized tasks of urban government. A multiplicity of elective offices, with little co-ordination or even co-operation among them; low salaries and low qualification for office and employment; a great deal of part-time government; patterns of petty, personal politics; almost complete absence of modern budgetary, accounting, and personnel practices; and very little attention or understanding from the press or the public—these are hardly the characteristics of effective urban management.

As urban functions have come crowding in on the counties, two plans of action have become distinguishable. First, to keep the new function or activity (where it is a new one) from the hands of the largely unqualified, existing officialdom, *ad hoc* boards or special units or agencies have been created; the distinction between a new special unit of government with its boundaries following those of the county, on the one hand, and a new department or agency of the county government, with practically complete autonomy from the rest of the governmental machinery, is often hard to discern. Second, the machinery of the old units has been gradually modified and transformed. New methods and practices come in slowly, but they do come in. The highway department finally gets an engineer; the courts acquire probation officers and social workers; the punched card is substituted for the heavy bound ledger; civil service systems are introduced. Sometimes, and usually toward the end of the process of change, the central decision-making machinery itself is transformed. The county board becomes a real policy-making, legislative, politically responsible body. Some form of central executive leadership is introduced. In California, where the urbanized county is perhaps most advanced, the county administrators are as powerful and as professionalized as are city managers, and in New York state, where the patterns are somewhat different but the needs are similar, the elected county executive is a tremendously influential, central, political figure.

In addition to adjustments in the corporate units and in the territorial units of local government, another important set of changes is occurring in the shifting mix of the marble cake of American federalism. Federal and state participation is going deeper and more pervasively into the sphere of local government responsibilities.

In terms of money spent, the three biggest functions of local government are schools, roads, and welfare. Federal and state participation in welfare operations has been decisive ever since the New Deal legislation of the thirties. Perhaps the real question here is whether or not significant *local* participation can be retained. More and more of the burden of the care for the aging is shifting to social security from old age assistance; if the provision for medical care for the aged is ever incorporated into the federal social security program, as the Kennedy administration advocates, the comparative weight will go even further in the federal direction. But our welfare needs, like our economic wants, are unlimited, and the way of the future will almost certainly involve a high degree of participation by all three levels. Certainly there will be recurring local efforts to throw off part of the yoke of high-level policy determination.

With federal ninety percent–ten percent matching money for the major freeways, and somewhat differing types and subdivisions of federal aid for other road projects, the inter-level mix in road matters is likely to become even more complex. And in the third major enterprise, education, while no general program of federal aid to education exists as yet, the opponents of federal aid can lose this battle only once, and they are likely to lose it on some future battleground or another. Already those who seek financial support for public education have discovered that it is less difficult to try to turn the spigot once, at the state level, than to attempt to turn it 67, or 92, different times—once in each county or school district. They are anxious to apply the same logic to federal-state relations in educational finance.

Perhaps even more interesting is the growing concern of both federal and state governments with functions which were once considered peculiarly appropriate for municipal action, since they relate to the shape and pattern of local urban land settlement. The fields of housing, planning, urban land controls, and mass transit are no longer merely municipal. Federal public housing and urban renewal programs are well entrenched and expanding; and there are state programs in both these fields in the more urbanized states. Both federal and state governments will assist local communities in urban planning. The new federal housing bill provides federal aid for the acquisition of urban open spaces. Federal and state concern with urban transit grows apace and the Advisory Commission on Intergovernmental Relations recommended that many federal grants for local public works be made only on the condition of active metropolitan-wide planning.

With a complex, interlaced mixture of local units —corporate, territorial, and special purpose—and with a good many structural and political elements of resistance to rationalization and reorganization of units, and with a growing pattern of state, federal, and local involvement in the same functions, the needs and opportunities for co-operative efforts and approaches are great. Contracts and agreements and understandings between different units are frequently made and even more frequently proposed. The currently attractive bauble, and perhaps one with great potential usefulness, is a co-ordinating council or conference of local officials representing many different units. A program of "massive co-operation" between governmental jurisdictions in the area of Salem, Oregon, attracted nation-wide attention. The New York Metropolitan Regional Council, the Association of Bay Area Governments, the Supervisors' Inter-County Committee in the Detroit area, the Washington Metropolitan Regional Conference, a new one just established in the Philadelphia area, and others springing up over the country, have many potentialities. They are apt either to avoid or to founder upon the difficult problems where interests differ radically since, without coercive powers, they are confronted with a Security Council veto-type situation. But co-operation and mutual exhortation may be useful in many other areas. The leagues and associations of cities and counties, both state and national, have been especially inclined to favor these devices for co-operation. Their preference for these arrangements is understandable; the emphasis on voluntary action preserves the identity and freedom of the constituent units.

Although I have already ventured some general comments on the adjustments and transformations occurring in the patterns of urban local government, perhaps the most sweeping generalization I can make is this: that these changes have occurred on the basis of step-by-step, incremental, *ad hoc* adjustments made to answer specific needs and forces and demands, and not on the basis of adherence to any general doctrine. They have come individually, a small piece, a fraction at a time. Victor Jones has called the process "creeping *ad hoc-ism*."

The clearest expression of this functional, piece-by-piece approach is the creation of special districts or special authorities to handle particular tasks. When a need appears for a new service, or a service is conducted on a geographical level not previously involved, the easiest approach seems to be to tailor-make a unit for these specific purposes. A port authority, or a transit authority, or a special metropolitan drainage district, or a small water district or sewer district to serve an area not now adequately served, seems the best, quickest, and easiest way to get the job done. Sometimes the *ad hoc* consideration does not require a new unit of government, but involves merely shifting some function from one level to another. More often, it means an even slower, less dramatic adjustment than this. A higher level of government provides a degree of financial aid, or technical assistance. A county-wide tax for the support of local school corporations is levied, to mitigate slightly the inequalities of tax resources. This tax grows, and along with it come some county-wide "standards." The same process occurs with regard to other functions and other units. This financial aid, or this technical assistance, or the area-wide standards, grow and spread and become more significant with time. Transformations in the character and tone of administration come even more unobtrusively and slowly. The growing professionalization of a particular agency or office may not be apparent at a particular point in time, but it accumulates a great force over the years.

The special significance frequently attached to the virtue of planning on a large-area basis is worthy of mention. The activities and output of specialized planning agencies have not carried much weight with the actual political decision-makers in most cases. Nevertheless, planning seems to involve research and rationality and an effort to balance and weigh different needs against each other and thus it seems especially desirable and attractive to persons who are worried about the complexity of our rather confused local government arrangements. Metropolitan-wide planning agencies appear, then, to be a peculiarly high-priority need. In one fashion or another they have been created in many of the country's metropolitan areas.

Although the changes and adjustments come piecemeal and without any particular doctrinal coherence, it does seem clear that providing more services for larger areas is the general trend. While new, small units (either special or general-purpose) are sometimes created to forestall the extension of larger-area activities, they are much more commonly created to provide services which did not heretofore exist, or which had to be provided by the individual householder or citizen for himself. The motive, even in these new small units, seems then more often than not to be one of providing a larger area for service. And, certainly, as functions shift from one unit to another, as territorial units enter into functions not previously conducted by them, and as large-scale *ad hoc* units are created to provide area-wide services—or at least to provide for an area wider than before—all these adjustments seem to form a clear pattern showing the locus of government and public policy-making and the administration shifting to larger areas and units. This does not mean that as the tide of urbanization swells and spreads, small units are abandoned, or that they are less important. The population is spreading over the countryside faster than thc growth of large units can handle the services for it. If, by great oversimplification, these transitional movements can be viewed as a continual shift of services and activities from individuals to small local units to larger units, it may be suggested that the pipeline is still being filled at entry about as fast as the shift is occurring.

Can any generalizations be made concerning the forces impelling such shifts toward larger areas, whether of functions moved to larger units, or of new, larger, *ad hoc* units created, or of a higher level of government entering into an area, or expanding its activities in an area? What, in other words, are the salient criteria affecting these shifts to larger units? Several may be suggested:

1. *Economies of scale.* While an increase in size of operations does not infallibly lower per unit costs in all governmental functions, in some instances it certainly does. For example, it would be costly technological nonsense to have more than one major airport for even a substantial urban region; a large general hospital should seldom be duplicated; when water must be brought a great distance, a single system for its accumulation and transportation is almost mandatory. It might be not only economically but technically impossible to duplicate a large-scale engineering enterprise to take the water out of Lake Michigan to flush sewage down the Illinois River. In instances such as these the lodging of a function with a large-area unit, whether general or special, is highly likely. The more economies of scale can be demonstrated, the more likely is a shift to a larger unit.

2. *Spillover effect.* When a governmental function or activity—or the problem which gives rise to the function—cannot be confined within specific geographical units, but has effects which spill over much wider areas, shift to a larger unit is likely. The most obvious example is the control of air pollution. The inspection of milk supplies is another. Water pollution is still another; the basis for the creation of a new metropolitan governmental unit in the Seattle area was the fact that no one of the

adjoining communities could control the pollution of Lake Washington. Of course, nearly all governmental functions have some of this spillover effect.[5] This is why gradual shifts continue in connection with most such functions.

3. *Crisis.* When a service or function is being conducted tranquilly and without disturbance or flap, there is little motive for change. But when bankruptcy is imminent, or when shortages are discovered or mismanagement is disclosed or when some kind of spectacular shortcoming produces public attention, then opportunity for reorganization and change occurs.

4. *Multi-level participation.* Where more than one layer or level of government—city, county, state, or federal—is involved in a function, the shift from smaller to larger unit is more easily accomplished. Less new ground needs to be broken, and fewer new agencies or departments created. In this kind of setup some of the balance of gravity in a particular functional domain may be conveniently shifted to the larger-unit level. Furthermore, where state or federal government participation is involved, their requirements and standards are such as to encourage, if not coerce, the smallest units to rely more and more on larger ones. For example, if it is feasible the federal government ordinarily prefers to channel its grants through an active state agency, rather

[5] I have borrowed this term from Harvey E. Brazer, "Some Fiscal Implications of Metropolitanism," in Guthrie S. Birkhead (ed.), *Metropolitan Issues* (Syracuse: The Maxwell Graduate School of Citizenship and Public Affairs, 1962).

than to work directly with individual cities or counties. And the state, in dealing with local school systems, almost inevitably tends to enhance the role of larger units.

5. *Professionalization.* The larger the governmental jurisdiction involved, the more likely the administrative service to become professionalized. Larger units encourage more specialization, more need for training, more career opportunities, more invitations to professionalism. Conversely, in professionalized services the push for higher-level administration is stronger, partly because of the opportunities for further professionalization seen by the bureaucracy, partly because the professionalized bureaucrats strive for uniformity across governmental jurisdictions, and find they can best get it by working with fewer and larger units.

The most impressive systematic movement toward larger governmental units in this country has come in public school administration. The first official Census of Governments, in 1942, reported more than 150,000 units of government in the United States; the Census of Governments which was taken in 1962 found substantially less than 100,000 units. This decrease has occurred entirely through a spectacular reduction in the number of independent school districts in the country. In 1942, 108,579 independent school districts were reported; in 1962 there were only 34,678.[6] Eighty percent of the re-

[6] 1962 Census of Governments, "Governmental Units in 1962" (preliminary report No. 6, released Dec. 6, 1962), p. 1.

duction occurred in a group of a dozen states in the heart of the country with the addition of New York. Large-scale shifts to larger units are still being made: in the last five years the number of independent school districts has been reduced by over thirty percent, and the number of all public school systems, which includes those systems operated by general purpose units of government, has decreased nearly as much.

These shifts to larger school systems have been made to secure economies of scale, a higher degree of equity through spreading the cost of education over larger tax bases, and, perhaps most important, to secure better quality programs obtainable only in larger units.

A variety of techniques have been used to secure these reorganizations. First and fundamental has been state financial assistance and supervision in programs which have involved a larger constituency and brought the powers and political concern of the state to bear more clearly upon the situation. Various elements of equalization have been injected into the state aid programs, which have highlighted the differences and inequities of school programs, and placed some of the burden of trying to lessen these differences upon the state as a whole. State legislation has been enacted to facilitate voluntary consolidation of school units, and to discourage division and formation of new ones. (With regard to municipal government in general, this is the stage into which a few state governments are beginning to venture, tentatively.) Then, a good many states have offered fiscal incentives for consolidations; through state programs of financial aid, carrots and sticks have both been supplied—the formulae for distribution of state aid have been juggled to reward consolidated districts and to punish small districts refusing to consolidate. Bills have been pushed through state legislatures requiring surveys and master-plans for school-district reorganization. The home-rule unit has been shifted, providing for county-wide, or large district-wide, vote on consolidation plans, without separate majorities in each existing unit. In a few instances states have resorted to actual compulsion, dissolving small units and consolidating them with others even without the approval or consent of their residents.

How have these very impressive reorganizations and shifts to larger units been politically possible? The same shifts in population, and the same technological changes in transportation and communication apply to many other functions of local government, yet vested interests, structural resistances, built-in veto powers, and non-rational reactions have made adjustments and reorganization affecting other functions move at a much slower pace.

The schools are characterized by some very significant, distinguishing features which, acting on the political environment, can lead to more thorough-going adjustments. The educational bureaucracy is very large and thoroughly professionalized. The ties of most teachers to the profession are stronger than to the local community, and this is particularly true of the professional leadership, where career patterns frequently involve many opportunities for lateral movement. This highly professionalized bureaucracy provides a national sharing of experiences and value goals through a generally respected intellectual leadership. From their conception in Teachers College, Columbia University, some of the devices for school reorganization spread rapidly over the country. The professional goals of better output, higher status for teachers, and higher salaries all combined to push in the direction of larger school units and generally prevailed over parochial loyalties to small communities and existing school jurisdictions. This bureaucracy is strongly organized into a very powerful interest group. It is numerous and pervasive, having substantial numbers of active, interested, intelligent members in every legislative constituency; its past record of political successes has built support for it within its own membership and has gained political respect for it from those outside, including politicians. It is nearly always supplied with very capable professional staff leadership. In the movements for larger school units, the bureaucratic interest group has had strong alliances with taxpayer groups, who have hopes of securing some economies of scale in a function where costs have been mounting rapidly. The long tradition of a high degree of state involvement in the function makes state inducement and manipulation and even coercion of local program and organization familiar and not unexpected. The vested interests who oppose shifts to larger units have included very few elected, paid local officials. (It is often elected, paid local officials, with extremely high personal involvement and extremely high political activism, who can exercise effective veto powers upon any other governmental reorganizations.)

Some aspects of the political environment of public education which have made possible massive changes in the system of units here have been suggested; now, how does the political environment surrounding *other* governmental functions compare? There are many differences, and some similarities. In other governmental domains, the economies of scale are not usually so clear, particularly because general purpose governmental units have many more functions. The vested interest in older organizational patterns appears to be substantially stronger in most other units than in public education. Certainly, most other functional bureaucracies are less professionalized; their occupational and career patterns are much more localized; most of the members of the bureaucracy see their interest in retaining existing systems, rather than shifting to larger units. Insofar as their bureaucracies are organized into interest groups, they tend to oppose, not to favor, governmental and functional reorganization, though there are some exceptions, largely in the more professionalized groups, such as social workers and public health workers. In many of the other functions, there is much less state involvement, and less motivation for active state concern about reorganization.

In spite of the differences between other functions and education, many of the same pressures for change exist, and, on a rudimentary scale, some of the same techniques and political resources are used. As state aid grows, and as it involves greater degrees of equalization among local units, pressures for rationalization of service areas increase. It has ordinarily been because of prodding at the state level that welfare, road administration, and public health have moved to larger units, commonly the county. The state has begun to apply to other functions some of the techniques first used on the schools. For example, in order to encourage devices for inter-local co-operation and municipal annexations, and discourage further growth and proliferation of new, small units, the state adopts policies which somewhat deter the formation of new municipal corporations and, in some instances, certain types of special districts. There have certainly been a considerable number of surveys of local governmental arrangements, and state governments are participating more actively in these studies. To facilitate some types of consolidations, a tendency to shift the home-rule base is appearing, so that not so many separate majorities will be required. The idea that state action alone, without consulting the local voter, could accomplish any drastic reorganization of local government units would be shocking in most American states, but the new metropolitan governments in Toronto and Winnipeg were adopted by provincial legislatures without referenda, and these incidents have not gone completely unnoticed in this country.

The bits and pieces of change mount up. The creation of new cities is limited and discouraged; in a few states existing cities make vigorous efforts to keep up with the spread of urbanization by annexation; the activities of existing cities are less and less confined by their corporate boundaries. The urban counties take on many of the aspects and functions of cities; their governments are slowly changed to conform to new responsibilities. New, larger special districts are formed. State and federal involvement increases. And especially functional responsibilities continually move to larger units.

No sweeping, rational, dramatic response to the twin drives of urbanization and urban dispersal has occurred. But the bits and pieces and segments add up to a very substantial and significant total of changes in the nature and character of the government for urban areas.

Chapter 5

THE URBAN
POLITICAL MARKETPLACE

DIFFERENT SOCIETIES HAVE DIFFERENT PATTERNS OF settlement characteristic of their differences in style of life. To the ancient Greeks the city-state was the standard spatial relationship between man and society; it was basic to their ways of thinking and acting. In medieval Britain the manor constituted the characteristic settlement pattern, and closely similar arrangements were spread throughout the feudal world. For centuries, the agricultural village has shaped and dominated the lives of most inhabitants in much of the Orient. And in America through the nineteenth century, the detached family-sized farm was the most characteristic habitation, one which served to transmit the influences of the frontier considered so influential by Frederick Jackson Turner and others. A growing minority of the population lived in cities, which were clearly distinguished from the rural areas. In America today and for the easily foreseeable future the characteristic pattern of settlement apparently is the single-family detached house on a paved street or road in an urbanized but not concentrated environment. The term "city" certainly does not adequately describe the area or region in which these homes are located, for reasons which have been suggested earlier. The term "metropolis" may be somewhat better but is still not quite accurate, since most of the same environmental factors are at work even in the smaller centers of settlement.

The historic model of American local government, as it was outlined in the second chapter of this book, made a clear distinction between corporate governments—those of cities—and territorial governments —those imposed by the state on all of its territory, such as counties and similar units. Corporate governments were considered the chief expression of local self-government, for it was these units which tackled the great range of services and activities required by people living closely together. This model fit nineteenth century America very well. Some of the formations and modifications of this pattern, based upon transformations in the society, have been described and discussed in the preceding chapter. Can a newer and more accurate model now be suggested?

The territorial units must certainly be a major component of a new model. Since they cover all of the land, they are always available to regulate or to provide service to a citizen wherever he may live. Furthermore, while some of the thickly settled urban regions overlap two or more counties, in a great many instances the county satisfactorily encompasses enough of the area to perform adequately at least most of the necessary local functions. Great variations will occur, of course, from state to state, and even within a state, but it seems likely that increasingly the center of responsibility for performing a great range of local government activities will gradually be shifted from cities to counties. Those who doubt this frequently point to the growing number of metropolitan areas (though still a minority) which spread across county lines and suggest that counties cannot adequately govern these metropolitan complexes. This may be true, but it also seems plausible to suggest that two or three or four counties form a more manageable universe of general governing agencies than do the twenty or thirty or fifty cities which ordinarily now exist within these sprawling urban giants.

Overlaying this basic network of territorial units will be a great many kinds of associational arrangements through which various groups of people, who may or may not be geographically defined, will co-operate to secure their particular goals. Many of these arrangements will constitute special districts. Most special districts will be for a single purpose; some will have more than one purpose, but the more purposes involved, the more difficult the organization, since the constituencies interested in the differing purposes may be radically disparate. A variety of contracts and co-operative agreements will also be made, to accomplish a great many functions. Geographical limits will be significant for some of these arrangements, and not for others. Fire protection may be provided within one area on the basis of tax support, within another area on the basis of contractual fees for services. Water utilities and sewage disposal services will be extended in response to a market which is partly economic and partly political. The line between public and private arrangements will probably become even more blurred than it now is. A government-operated electric utility, an electrical co-operative, and a privately-owned utility with government regulation even now provide an interesting spectrum of arrangements. The provision of public transit services by "privately-owned" corporations, which have public subsidies, and to areas which overlap various governmental jurisdictions, is an example of a complex public-private association. Many of the associations will be between governmental units, both special purpose and general purpose. One of the most pervasive of the types of co-operative arrangements will involve several levels of government—federal, state, and local. Some of these co-operative "agreements" will include elements of coercion and compulsion by higher governmental levels, but the distinction between compulsion, coercion, inducement, and permission will probably become even more blurred than it is now.

Viewed in this light, the municipal corporation becomes just one variety of associational arrangement, a sort of multi-purpose special district, with some of its purposes and functions applying to all persons living within a specified limit, some to only portions of the citizenry within these limits, and some to interested customers or participants in an area overlapping the geographical limits of the unit.

If the suggested model has any accuracy, where is the clearly defined self-governing community? It certainly is not the traditional central city, which is largely being lost in a jumble of other units and arrangements. It is hardly to be found in new satellite suburban communities, which serve some purposes and functions but not enough. A new metropolitan-wide, self-governing community is likely to be a will-o'-the-wisp in most circumstances, beckoning the crusader, but rarely if ever attained. The substructure existing now in the territorial units, primarily counties, will hardly serve as the vehicle for truly integrated communities, particularly because the territorial boundaries are largely immutable and frequently have only coincidental relationships to the areas of denser settlement.

This suggested model for local government recognizes that most Americans are in reality members of many overlapping communities, and that it is difficult if not impossible to attach their communal loyalties to a single unit of local government. This is a mobile, shifting society where a man sleeps in one locality, works in another or in several different localities, finds his recreation and much of his social interaction in perhaps still another, is frequently involved with New York and Washington and Chicago as central business districts, and is as likely to put down roots in a corporation or a profession as in a locality. Community does not mean the same thing as it might have in medieval Britain, or in the nineteenth century Middle West, or in the Philadelphia of the carriage and the streetcar. In India the term "community" may be applied to a religious grouping, and in Africa to a tribal grouping more strongly than to the modern national state; so, in America, where patterns of urban living spread over the landscape, "community" is hardly unitary, and self-government must probably be as complex as are our interrelationships.

This recognition that simple, clear-cut definitions and arrangements can probably not be attained should not frighten us. Current thinking and scholarship about the American federal system has developed the theory that neat, clear, simple divisions of power between governments are neither accurate, achievable, nor desirable. Just as in the nation's relationships with the states, one cannot say to the other "you take this function, and I will take that one," and "you stay on your side of the fence, and I will stay on mine," so area and function at the local level cannot be clearly, simply, and logically allocated. Just as federalism seems to be advanced in theory and practice when we abandon arguments about division of power and concern ourselves more with arrangements for division of labor, so may the study of local government make progress when we concern ourselves somewhat less with jurisdictions and powers and somewhat more with co-operative arrangements and piecemeal shifts of responsibility.

All of these governmental arrangements—territorial units, corporate units, special districts, cooperative understandings, mechanisms for state and federal participation—are involved in a pluralistic political marketplace in which influence is the primary medium of exchange. Individuals and groups have varying needs and wants, and they try to satisfy these needs and wants through whatever governmental machinery is available. If the pressures for a particular action meet too much resistance in one channel, another may be tried; if the institutional arrangements do not provide appropriate channels, and the force is strong enough, the institutional arrangements will be modified.

Ordinarily the institutional arrangements and procedures at any particular time tend to give special weight to the status quo and resist innovation and change. Is it correct to say that the more complex and pluralistic the institutional arrangements, the more resistance to change? In his study of political influence in Chicago, Edward Banfield concluded that "the wider the distribution of authority, the larger the stock of power that is required if proposals are to be adopted" and "as the number of autonomous actors in a situation increases, the probability of adoptions decreases."[1] Two things may be said to counter this hypothesis that increasing governmental complexity (which we certainly appear to have) increases the weight of veto powers and de-

[1] Edward C. Banfield, in *Political Influence* (Glencoe, Ill.: The Free Press, 1961), p. 318.

creases the likelihood for innovation. First, though a great number of governmental units or agencies may affect the interests of an individual, not all of them are concerned with each action involving him. They certainly overlap and interact in some measure, but there is a great deal of specialization; and action, even innovation, can frequently be secured without having to touch many bases. Second, all government combined occupies a comparatively small portion of the attention and involvement of most Americans. If any particular actor, or group of actors, is sufficiently concerned about securing action from government to make a reasonably heavy investment in effort and influence, there is strong likelihood that comparable but contrary investment of attention and influence will not be forthcoming from any potential opposition.[2] While the institutional machinery may have the potentiality of a brake, the brakes are likely to be applied only when important interests might be seriously threatened by the contemplated action. I must confess that these two observations constitute only marginal qualifications to the generalization that the more elaborate the system of units and agencies, the more difficult innovation may be.

The great variations in the character of units and of constituencies result in great variations in the nature of the political process within them. The areal

[2] Chapters 24, 25, and 26 of Robert Dahl, *Who Governs?* (New Haven: Yale University Press, 1961), expand and elaborate this theme.

differentiation of geographical sections of urban areas will greatly affect their political behavior. Although the current immigrants to the older central cities apparently do not respond to exactly the same political tactics as some of their immigrant predecessors, the role of political party and of strong ward and precinct organization and of various kinds of personal loyalty may be much stronger in the central cities than elsewhere. Certainly the influence of Negroes and other ethnic groups will be more noticeable and pronounced. To middle-class and upper middle-class sections, businesslike methods and procedures will be very attractive, with part-time boards of directors, or councils, or trustees turning full-time operations over to hired professional managers. Many of the special purpose districts, in particular, will be actually run by a very small group of interested activists.

The most difficult adjustments, and the slowest, will accompany the transformation of the counties and a few of the townships, as they take on the responsibilities of urban services and have to try to fit these activities into the small-scale, rather personal, politics inherited from their rural forebears.

The role of political parties is certain to vary widely. In some cases, where an active party organization has a strong foothold in some key segments of the governmental machinery, a substantial portion of the decisional processes may occur through party channels. These instances, however, are likely to be more the exception than the rule. With proliferating special constituencies and absence of party cohesion in the various groups, party activities may be more concentrated on state and national affairs and on those particular units where small patronage spoils may be accumulated.

The blurring of the distinction between city and country has tended to blur the problem of apportionment of state legislatures. As the relative proportion of the population living in central cities is matched and passed by the proportion living in urbanized fringes, the cities are less underrepresented than they were. Furthermore, the cleavages between urban and non-urban representatives shift and change with the character of the issues.

The effect of these pluralistic governmental arrangements upon the net allocations of influence and power to different segments of the society will be hard to measure. Influence is an extremely difficult factor to identify clearly and even more difficult to measure.

As governmental units and agencies become specialized and in many instances relatively autonomous, the access and influence of persons with high interest and involvement in these particular areas is increased. Schoolteachers know that their influence is likely to be greater in an autonomous school unit than in a school system controlled by a general purpose government. Thus in their roles as specialists, individuals will have enhanced opportunities for access and participation; but in their roles as general citizens, they will be deterred. As the tendencies of men to specialize and to group themselves into limited communities lead to specialized and *ad hoc* governmental institutions, so the existence of these institutions tends to reinforce the position and influence and role of specialists and their interest groups.

It seems clear that the more complex the governmental arrangements, the greater the influence and role of governmental professionals, of experts, of career bureaucrats, whether within government or as staff members of interest groups. The more complicated the maze, the more expertness, the more experience, the more constant attention is required to thread a path through it. The involvement, for example, of several levels of government in public welfare programs or in urban renewal programs has helped produce a system of regulations and policies and understandings which can be negotiated only by professionals, or by those whose interests are so directly involved that they must invest the time and effort necessary to learn their way around.

Is there a power elite in these spreading urban regions, a discernible set of top influentials who determine most of the important matters? This possibility certainly has its attractions for those who doubt the desirability of public policies determined by the tugging and hauling and jockeying of special interest groups working through complexes of agencies and units; a single power structure, which could set priorities and reconcile goals, appeals to the desire for order and simplicity. Several sociologists who have studied community power structures have suggested that such a community influence elite exists, although others have doubted their hypothesis. The general thrust of the analysis undertaken here obviously runs in a contrary direction. Influence is certainly unequally distributed, and it may well be interesting to try, in any given community, to identify a certain number of people who are thought to have the greatest portions of it. But, if the nature of the community itself is becoming more complex and less definable and if the nature of the policy-determining institutions is similarly less simple and clear, more than likely the decisional elites also tend to be substantially fractured and differentiated. The field investigations of Dahl in New Haven and Banfield in Chicago tend to confirm this opinion.

Clearly, reliance upon a laissez-faire economic marketplace is diminishing; structure and control and institutional rigidities, and even central planning are becoming more prevalent in *economic* affairs. To suggest that the forces of technological and demographic change are tending to loosen and differentiate and make more complex the bargaining and negotiating and adjusting processes of local self-government may seem paradoxical. The national political marketplace, with the growth of clearer and better-organized national interest groups, the rise of executive leadership, and perhaps even a slight increase in party responsibility, may be moving somewhat in the direction of a clearer, simpler structuring.

But the evidence certainly suggests strongly to this observer that the contrary is true at the level of local government. Even the increased injection of national and state policies and administrative activities into local affairs seems to have tended to produce further specialization and differentiation and necessity for negotiation and bargaining instead of clarification, simplification, and integration. This bargaining, semi-competitive, political marketplace at the level of local government, of course, has a great deal of structuring, of institutionalization. It resembles Kenneth Galbraith's system of countervailing power more than it does the unstructured competition of Adam Smith or Herbert Spencer.

When I say that the processes of policy determination and application at local levels are conducted in a political marketplace—a marketplace where widely varying forces and special interests are occupied in a complex arena of governmental and private agencies and associations and units—I make no assumption that an invisible hand is working to produce an inevitable public interest.

In the absence of a postulated invisible hand, how can this urban political marketplace be evaluated? Can responsiveness, co-ordination, rationality be achieved in this environment?

Various types of responsiveness exist, and they operate through various channels. In specialized, fractionated, and pluralistic governmental institutions, the channels of political responsiveness to special and limited constituencies probably operate more effectively while responsiveness to a general electorate through general political channels is lessened.

In more and more fields of governmental activity, the general outlines of public policy are being debated and shaped in a national forum, while the specific applications and variations of these policies are local. In housing and transit and open space policy, in hospital construction and even in public education, the national forum, where general political responsibility to a general electorate seems somewhat clearer, participates, only partially it is true, but that partial participation tends to shape the general outlines of policy. The ordinary citizen, in his capacity as voter and general consumer of public services, tends to be confused and befuddled by this complicated sharing of public functions at the local level, and his sense of separation and alienation from local government is probably increasing. On the other hand, if he has a concrete, specific, and important interest—if he is a contractor who builds roads, or a dairyman whose milk is being inspected, he will know the appropriate paths of access, and his views will probably be heard, understood, and given a weight that is perhaps even greater than the abstract "public interest" would require.

As for co-ordination, this is hardly a value goal in itself, except in the sense of the attractiveness of order and symmetry. As Emerson put it, "A foolish consistency is the hobgoblin of little minds." In a world where values are relative, where the "right" policy is rarely certain, there is some utility in having a degree of variety and contradiction in the policies and approaches of different agencies and different units. In their approaches to public welfare programs in my own state, the county departments of public welfare are probably excessively personal and flexible. A friend of mine, on a recent visit to Russia, complained to the guide about what he considered to be the excessive consistency and uniformity of approach of the Russian press. On being told that in America ten different journals would have ten different stories and viewpoints on one matter, the guide replied that since there was only one truth, nine of them must be lying. Not being so certain of the truth, we prefer the ten journals. Since we are rarely certain of the "best" public policy, perhaps we should pause somewhat in our quest for policy co-ordination.

But whatever the virtues of variety and inconsistency in governmental programs, circumstances in which conflict and inconsistency are wasteful and inappropriate are certainly apparent. The political processes of exerting, comparing, and reconciling pressures and influence, even though they work in and through different institutional channels, will manage to resolve some of these differences. If one agency proposes to operate a public park on the same land through which another agency proposes to build a highway, some institutional machinery will be found, sooner or later, for some kind of decision on or reconciliation of the differing views. Without a central forum or political focus, these problems may be resolved slowly, haltingly, and occasionally not at all, but ordinarily ways will be found in which the relative weights of influence brought to bear in the political marketplace can be calculated, and the issues resolved.

Can we trust these processes which resolve the parallelograms of diverse political influences, through negotiation and discussion and calculation and occasional election, to help us achieve a better, more rational, more satisfying urban life? This question is one of the most difficult to speak to, since the *shape* of the "better place to live," the shape of the modern, urban City of God, is both disputable and disputed. If governmental institutions could be simplified and clarified we might gain a higher level of consideration and deliberation, a fuller and more precise posing of alternative choices, a more accurate appraisal of the probable causes and effects of present conditions and future policies, a more rational conclusion as to the "best" policy. We pay a price for our fluid, mobile society, for our substitution of multiple memberships in multiple communities for a single membership in a simple, integrated community. A lower level of rationality in public policy-making may be a part of the price.

There are many who will not be content with this description of a relatively chaotic and disorderly hodgepodge of local governing institutions and political forces. Some, of course, when confronted with a description of an even more complex and confusing society, are tempted to ask that the world be stopped so that they may get off. Many others, however, are willing to go along for the ride, seeing much of interest and excitement in it, but unwilling to concede or accept the notion that the city is withering away—the city as a definable, corporate community of friends and neighbors with common interests which can be furthered by integrated, unified political processes.

Several qualifications to this description of a gradually disintegrating city are obvious to any intelligent observer. First, in talking about the withering of the city, we are talking about a continued projection of present trends into the future. There is a lot of life in the old girl yet, and the legal and traditional roots of the concept of a unified, integrated, corporate, single, self-governing community are so deep and strong that, whatever the future trends, many of the historical forms and patterns will go on for a long time.

Second, the governmental machinery available in most cities is still, ordinarily, the strongest and most effective machinery available at the local level. This institutional resource is a valuable one and will tend to make cities more important participants in the local political process than their jurisdictional and demographic limitations would otherwise provide.

Third, there are ways in which the traditional city can be modified to increase its viability. One is by extensive use of compulsory or semi-compulsory annexation. To encompass the entire span of spreading urban patterns of living within city limits may not be possible but, in some circumstances, vigorous annexation policies may keep closely enough on the trail of the urban sprawl to provide a strong basis for reasonably general, reasonably integrated city government. But compulsory annexation is a transgression of the traditional model of the city as a *voluntary* incorporation, and political resistance to it is very strong in most states. Where it is pursued, the city becomes less a voluntary corporate grouping of citizens seeking their common goals and more an extension of the power of the state over particular territory. Or the city can accept a role as provider of various services, extraterritorially, on the basis of agreement and contract and understanding. This role is a valuable and continuing one, but hardly the traditional role of the city.

Fourth, the goal of a unified, corporate community is so attractive that a great deal of loyalty and support will continue to be attached to it, whether in defense of existing cities, in attempts to create new cities in the fringes, or in continued efforts to construct new, large, metropolitan governmental communities. These are noble ambitions, often admirable and commendable. Such efforts will certainly have some successes. To suggest that the probabilities are against a high percentage of success is not to decry the efforts.

Strong as are these forces for retaining some, at least, of the patterns of the past, the continuing adaptation of governmental forms and institutions to spreading urbanization will probably involve more and more of the *ad hoc,* piecemeal, partial, and pluralistic devices and adjustments instead of simple, clean, integrated responses. As we adapt our institutions to our changing styles of life, it seems likely that both the sense of community and the governmental arrangements for communities will become more fluid and more diverse than they have been in the past.

INDEX